"Children who read this book could have their lives changed forever. The book itself… the story Robert has to tell… can build up any young person's self esteem because they can relate to the trials and tribulations Robert endured. Put this book in their hands, and something magical can happen. You'll watch our youth envision their true potential. Put this book in their hands, and you'll watch them soar."

—HON. LINDA CHAPA LAVIA
ILLINOIS HOUSE OF REPRESENTATIVES, 83RD DISTRICT
CHAIRPERSON, APPROPRIATIONS COMMITTEE-ELEMENTARY &
SECONDARY EDUCATION

"This book has taught me that even though I'm small, I can hold a big place in this world. Also I have learned that there are no shortcuts on the road of life and if I take a wrong turn there is always a way to get back on track. I love this book and plan to read it again and again!"

—SARAH BAILEY 11 YEARS OLD

"[Barrio] is not only an eye opener, but is geared to everyone, for most of us are not born with a silver spoon in our mouth. It's about life experiences and how to overcome any defeat by having strength and faith. It should be read by all teens to let them know that we have choices in our lives and can make no excuses for our failures."

—SONIA VARELA
HISPANIC LIAISON, ILLINOIS SECRETARY OF STATE

"The *From the Barrio* book and curriculum helps young people establish their identity, determine core values, decide what is truly important to them and helps them develop a vision for their future. The end result we are seeing is that students participating in the program are developing the critical thinking skills necessary for academic achievement, as well as self-regulation and discipline."

—CARL HURDLIK
CHICAGO PUBLIC SCHOOLS, COMMUNITY RELATIONS

"Robert Renteria carved an innovative path by trying to eliminate— with high intensity—gangs, drug activities and other crimes among our youth. His unselfish approach of presenting his life story through his books and challenging workshops and lectures, has exploded with tremendous accolades in schools, churches and youth detention centers throughout the nation! Read the book."

—**GUILLERMO "BILL" PEREZ**
2009 CHICAGO LATINO PROFESSIONAL OF THE YEAR

"From the Barrio to the Board Room and the From the Barrio Foundation are able to bring meaningful change to the classroom because they have created a living document to describe and explain what it means to understand poverty, gang related activities, drugs, and antisocial behavior with a strong message that hard work, persistence, and education can make a difference in the lives of our youth."

—**DR. LOUISE EGGERT-NEVINS**
RAPID RESPONSE SPECIALIST
CHICAGO PUBLIC SCHOOLS, OFFICE OF PRINCIPAL PREPARATION
AND DEVELOPMENT

"The first time I ever opened a *Barrio* book was at a meeting for a friend of mine who was running for Cook County sheriff. I was sitting in Mr. Renteria's office. Before I could get through the first chapter I saw something special. The deal was sealed for me later that evening when I got home and gave the book to my daughter, a fourteen year old freshman in Chicago Public Schools. She started reading it that night and I still haven't gotten my book back.

—**KORY BILBRO**
PREVENTION SPECIALIST, CHICAGO

"From the Barrio to the Board Room had a profound effect on me. It showed a strong message of hope and encouragement. There are choices that these teenagers make every single day and to many there is no light at the end of the tunnel. From the Barrio gives them that light, it shows them that they can follow their dream!"

—**TAMI PRINCIPE**
FOUNDER OF WOMENS RECREATION, INC.

FROM THE BARRIO
to the Board Room

FROM THE BARRIO
to the Board Room

ROBERT RENTERIA
As told to Corey Michael Blake

www.fromthebarrio.com
www.roundtablecompanies.com
Cover and interior design by Nathan Brown,
Writers of the Round Table Inc.
Interior layout by Sunny DiMartino

Printed and bound in the U.S.A.

ISBN: 978-1-61066-011-2

Library of Congress Control Number: 2008922376

Contents

Acknowledgments ix

Foreword xi

Introduction: Proud to be a Latino! xiii

Chapter 1   The Wonder Years: Growing Up Poor in East L.A. 1

Chapter 2   A Life-Changing Accident: I Became the Chosen One 13

Chapter 3   Gang Life: My Rebel Years in East L.A. 19

Chapter 4   The Military: No Racism, Everybody's Green 33

Chapter 5   Fire in My Belly: The Climb to Corporate America 41

Chapter 6   Corporate America: Keeping Up With the Big Boys 55

Chapter 7   The Dream: Being My Own Boss 71

Afterword   You, Too, Can Chase the American Dream! 83

Epilogue 93

From the Barrio Foundation 103

ACKNOWLEDGMENTS:

Sometimes people think that there are certain things we should not talk about because they're forbidden, inappropriate or politically incorrect. This story and this book, although it has my name on it, this is not the Robert Renteria story. This is your story, this is our story, this is the story of people all around the world who come from various barrios and ghettos, who come from tough places and who struggle daily to pay their bills, feed their families and do whatever they need to do—legally mind you—to come out clean on the other side.

This is a story about hope and dreams, about believing in you and also about believing in God. You see, even though we can't see God we still believe, and that my friends is called faith. Faith to be anybody you want to be, and that's exactly what we are going to be talking about.

Having been stabbed, shot at, a drug seller and a drug doer, I changed the direction of my life to become a successful business owner. Now I want to reach out—not only to help others look deep within themselves to find the courage, imagination, belief, answers and direction they need in their lives, but to help them to chase the American dream. (It's your God given right!)

I want to give a sincere thanks to my mother for giving me life and helping me to understand that if you see it you can be it. And for teaching me that the most important thing in this life is family, that you protect it, respect it and you don't abuse the privilege (I love you). My gratitude goes to my grandfather and grandmother who took us in as children and who were always there to share their unconditional love and wisdom (Rest in peace). To my uncle, Armando—without you my life might likely have been history—thank you, brother, for always being there and watching my back. My two sisters, Lori and Regina, you both mean the world to me, and to my only niece Lauren—I am so proud of you for pursuing your education and for being the first in our family to be graduating from college. To my dear friend Ben Haney, who with nothing to gain, unselfishly opened doors for me so that I could have the opportunity to show what a poor little boy from East L.A. could do in corporate America if given a chance. The Dream Team, all of the sales professionals who helped me climb that broken ladder of corporate America (who loves you, baby!). You will forever be my band of brothers.

To all the vendors and suppliers who did look out for me in the business world, I promise you, I will leave this dance with those who helped me get here. To all my past and current customers who have supported me throughout my sales career, you are all the most important people in my business life. Thank all of you for helping me to get "From the Barrio to the Board Room."

To my publisher and friend Corey Michael Blake, thank you for the incredible job you did in capturing my words to explain that in this day and age, Hispanics or otherwise are no longer content with living a mediocre lifestyle or being the underdog. After decades and decades, we are defying the odds and going for the gold.

Lastly, I would like to bow my head, get on my knees and give thanks to the almighty God for giving me the strength and fortitude to hang in there and for blessing me with so many wonderful people who have helped and extended themselves to me personally.

—ROBERT J. RENTERIA JR.

FOREWORD:

Robert Renteria's story needs to be heard. Young people are living in neighborhoods with more violence than ever before and gangs have become a routine part of the environment. For some of our young people, survival is all they know. We have to show them that there is more. We have to encourage them to look beyond, and have a sense of the future and look to where they want to be 10 or 20 years from now. Robert clearly illustrates that life is full of choices, and the choices you make will determine which way you go.

From the Barrio to the Board Room shows young people that others who were just like them, with similar experiences, have made something positive happen in their lives. How did we do this? Both Robert and I were able to disconnect from our environment to a certain degree so that we could not only continue to survive within it, but also look toward the future. Our personal experiences gave us the upper hand in dealing with gangs, violence, drug and alcohol abuse and our youth dropping out of school. We are committed to our community because we recognize that many of these young men and women need role models and individuals who can nurture and mentor them.

This is the message that Robert and I have in common. We've been there, yet here we are. We made it out from the Barrio and our kids can do the same. But the Barrio should stay with us as a reminder of who we are. I always say that you can take me out of the Barrio but you can't take the Barrio out of me. I also say that although I am the first Latina in the State Senate, I won't be the last!

When I visit schools I tell young people that education is the most precious gift that you can give yourself and your community. By becoming educated, you can understand the social injustice and economic issues that exist out there. What you capture in the classroom is something that nobody can ever take away from you. And you can choose to make it a positive experience!

A book like Robert's can make a difference and change the course of someone's life because it is a story that hits home. *From the Barrio* tells you that it does not matter where you are born, what community you grow up in, or where in society you may be; what matters is you and what you want to do with your life. Everything that Robert has shared—the words, his commitment and his philosophy—is a reality. He is living proof that a kid from the Barrio can make it, and his story will change lives.

—THE HONORABLE IRIS Y. MARTINEZ
ILLINOIS STATE SENATOR

INTRODUCTION: PROUD TO BE A LATINO!

The first eleven years of my sales career were quite a whirlwind, and I refer to the ride as being on a subway—everything was moving so fast that it was just a blur! I look back now, coming from the barrio of East L.A., and can honestly say that I made it "FROM THE BARRIO TO THE BOARD ROOM."

For me, "corporate America" was a breeding ground for mediocrity, and I spent too much of my life chasing the dream of being an executive, only to find that—in the end—it was not at all like I hoped it would be. The politics, the bureaucracy and the posturing, along with constantly having to watch my back for the guy or gal who was bucking for my position, was less than desirable. It was like swimming in a pool of anarchy.

I believe that you need to give back to those who help build your business, and corporate America just didn't think that way. Many organizations hire from the outside because a candidate has a college degree or graduated from a business school (as if that qualifies the person for the job), when the company probably already has the best person for the position in place and currently doing a large part of that job.

In the early 1960s, only four percent of Latinos graduated high school, and only two percent went on to college. Today, education for the Latino (the Hispanic-American) and all ethnicities is becoming the great equalizer that cuts across gender, color, religion and national origin. The memories of welfare, drugs, discrimination, crime, alcohol, unemployment and under-employment, gangs, violence and all other obstacles (or, should I say, perceived obstacles) are now being challenged by Hispanics all around the world.

All races who were once poor are building great successes and accomplishments globally and have obviously made a long overdue decision to come together, take the lead and draw from our roots to break through the barriers that have tried to boycott us from economic power.

We must truly believe in ourselves regardless of our background, economic position, language, length of our hair, color of our skin or gender. It comes down to the core values my mother taught me: "familia" (family) and "orgullo" (pride). Don't let where you came from dictate who you are, but let it be part of who you become.

The business world should be easier now than it was for me growing up as a Latino, but you still have to take advantage of every moment and every opportunity, and be willing to work harder than the next guy. There are those who say that some people were just at the right place at the right time. Maybe. But I believe that is only true if you actually do something about it once you are there.

Although the doors for me did not open easily, I applied my persistence and faith to guide me in the direction I wanted to go. Respectfully speaking, I proudly carried the burden on my shoulders throughout those eleven years that I was not just representing the industry or my family, but rather my entire race and other under privileged races as well. My intention for this book is to get it into the hands of as many young people as possible. If I can help a handful of them chase the American dream and break the cycle of poverty, I'll consider that a good start!

FROM THE BARRIO
to the Board Room

CHAPTER ONE

The Wonder Years: Growing Up Poor in East L.A.

I was born in the barrio East Los Angeles on October 13, 1960. My parents were factory laborers. Growing up in the early 1960s was a very humble time, and the focus was just on working, trying to pay the bills, and putting bread on the table. We lived in a stuffy single-room bachelor apartment with one small bed and a chest of drawers that my mother used as a bed for me. Our stove was a hot plate, and our entertainment consisted of either watching the big black hairy roaches climb the walls or my mother swatting flies with a rolled-up newspaper.

I never truly came to know my father, who abandoned us when I was only three years old. The only legacy he left our family was a pile of bills and a bunch of empty bottles of booze. In the end, the womanizing, drugs and alcohol would kill him at the young age of thirty-eight.

My mother had a very rough time during my infancy. She worked at many different factories at night and then took on small jobs in the early mornings to make additional money. She tackled jobs on weekends, such as painting and cleaning people's houses; she even did some janitorial work scrubbing floors and toilets.

My mother worked as many hours as the factory would allow her, which sometimes meant a double shift of sixteen hours. The minimum wage back then was a measly $1.25 per hour, and it was difficult for her to keep up with the finances, let alone keep any food in the house, especially while my father was still around. As a drug addict and an alcoholic, he would steal things—pawn or sell whatever we had of any value to buy drugs—but because my mother loved him immensely, she tried to keep this dark and humiliating side of our lives a secret by putting up with my father's addictions. There is no explanation as to why love allows you to tolerate someone else's unacceptable behavior.

My mother did not know when she got married that my father was doing drugs. She was very young, naive and smitten with his good looks and smooth-talking ways. My grandparents had sheltered her; she was raised believing in blue skies and butterflies and was clueless back then. Two or three months went by before she figured out what was going on. Eventually, she found vials of heroin and needles, wrapped in a plastic bag and hidden in the toilet tank and also taped behind the dresser. My mother was scared and too embarrassed (who wouldn't be?) to tell anyone about the heartache we were going through.

While pregnant with my little sister, my mother worked until she was about eight months along, hiding her stomach by wearing tight girdles and loose clothing. Back in those days, women were only allowed to legally work until they were five months pregnant, but my mother tried covering up her stomach as best she could and always found a means to make money. She took the bus to work or sometimes, if she had no money, walked the long and dreadful three-mile, lonely hike up and down those unsafe, dark and dirty streets.

Before my little sister was born, we were kicked out of our apartment because we could not pay the rent. Because she was so far along in her pregnancy, my mother had not been able to work, and my father, who was usually missing in action, was certainly not making up the difference. The landlord repossessed all of our belongings and put a deadbolt lock on the door. We were actually standing in the rain on the street with no money, soaked from head to toe, and with no place to go. My mother pleaded with the landlord, but he wasn't sympathetic to our cause and refused to listen to her problems.

It was then that my mother finally broke down and told my grandparents that we were literally homeless and broke with only the clothes on our backs to our name. My mother had a lot of pride and never wanted to ask for help because that's how we were taught, but we had hit rock bottom.

We moved in with my grandparents and uncle, who lived in East L.A. on Gage Avenue near City Terrace in a very small, old, rented one bedroom home. I stayed in a musty, concrete, dark and unfinished basement, sleeping on a dirty, smelly mattress on the floor where I could hear the mousetraps snapping throughout the night. I remember being scared, because I'd swear that sometimes I would be startled in the midst of a deep sleep, feeling the scratches of tiny feet running over my arm.

At about five years old, I walked up and down the neighborhood streets with my red wagon, knocking on doors and collecting empty soda bottles that I would turn in at grocery stores, where I was given refunds for the returned merchandise. This was how I helped the family make money, which I then gave to my mother to buy food and whatever else we needed. We were all somewhat deprived, but we were, without question, very close, and despite our struggles, Mom never allowed us, as a family, to be separated. I have seen plenty of other parents throw in the towel, give up, and turn their backs and simply walk away—but not my mom.

During the childhood years of my life, my father was constantly in and out of jail, all the while continuing to womanize and squander away money on heroin and alcohol. My mother, though, continued to work the evening shifts while my little sister, Lori, and I stayed with Grandpa and Grandma.

I recall my mother taking us shopping at thrift stores and getting many hand-me-downs from my older cousins. Most times, we looked like we dressed mismatched, but we had clothes on our backs and shoes on our feet, even though sometimes we had holes in the soles.

My mother was bound and determined that we would not live the lifestyle we had been born into. She said, "One day, no matter what sacrifices I need to make, we are all going to get out of this misery."

My extended family, although all mostly from California, did not live in East L.A. They did not have the bad run my mother did or maybe simply made better choices. When we saw them, everyone seemed close and nobody looked down at us or said anything stupid. That's why I always looked forward to the occasional Saturday afternoons at the park, visiting and playing games with my uncles, aunts and cousins. Among family, I could hold my head up and not feel lesser or belittled.

My mother was a very beautiful woman and a very clean person. She made sure that as long as we had soap and water, we were always impeccably clean regardless of what we wore. Even today, my appearance and my home are immaculate.

As a child, there was a very short period in our lives when my mother was not working and we paid for our groceries with food stamps. People looked at us and pointed their fingers, as if to say we were losers. I was just thankful that we had food, and I guess back then I was not embarrassed because I was probably too young to know any better.

In those days, we had no shower, only a tub, and no such thing as a washer or dryer. Eventually, Grandpa did locate a second-hand wringer washer for us, but we normally washed and rinsed our clothes by hand and then hung them outside to air dry on a clothesline. Breakfast usually consisted of puffed wheat cereal or oatmeal and sometimes scrambled eggs with chorizo or fried bologna. Lunch and dinner were usually Spam or beans, with Grandma making handmade flour tortillas and salsa. I still have strong memories of my mother diluting the milk with water into several containers so that we would have enough to go around—especially for my little sister. We ate lots of beans and tortillas for dinner. Fried beans, smashed beans, beans with chili, beans with *carne* (hamburger meat), beans boiled in a pot, beans with bacon, beans with weenies, bean juice, beans, beans and more beans! My mother also knew at least a dozen ways to cook Spam. I recall anxiously looking forward to the smell on Sunday mornings because we would occasionally have homemade *menudo* (tripe soup).

I remember being the only kid looking in the window of the local candy store, standing there with my mouth wide open while other children were buying and eating candy bars. Going to restaurants rarely happened either, but sometimes we walked several blocks down the street and hit one of the corner taco stands. I tell people all the time that we were so poor growing up, if someone broke into our house to rob us, we would have robbed him. I'm not kidding!

All of the men in my life were laborers, and almost all of the men in our family were alcoholics. Just about every night, my grandfather would quietly and privately sit in his bedroom drinking his Ripple or other cheap wines that he stashed under the bed. Out of respect, because I was a child, he never drank in front of me. Then my mother, who remarried when I was nine years old, married a man who later turned out to be a physically abusive heavy drinker.

My real father had been quite the ladies' man. A good-looking, suave guy with a fast tongue and quick zipper, my mother says that he was spit and polished head to toe. Even though there was little money back then, she recalls him always being dressed "to the nines." He was a man who was not responsible and probably not the kind of guy who was ever meant to be married. She tells me that when he was sober, he was simply great. She loved that he was charismatic, fun, exciting to be with, had an outgoing personality, could get down and play a mean trumpet and was liked by everyone. I believe that my mother carried her love for him throughout her life. I say this only because when we do talk about him, she always gets a twinkle in her eyes and smiles. So I know she loved him, indeed, even today.

My relationship with my stepfather was tough because he was neither an affectionate person nor one to compliment anyone for good efforts or a job well done. When my mother remarried, we moved into an old apartment complex that was more like "the projects" in today's standards—but it was home. He had me push-mow the lawn, keep up the garden, clean the house and garage, paint, wash his truck, shine his shoes and anything else that kept me busy and at home. For some reason, he did not want me involved in outside activities or having any friends, which was hard because, like other children, I wanted to play sports and have a social life.

My mother would sometimes argue with him about letting me go to a school dance or even participate in baseball or football. My mother got her way, and I eventually joined some leagues. Out of all the times I played, he only attended once and that was because, I believe, my mother made him go. I remember one year in junior high, I played at a father-son game and took my uncle. Don't get me wrong, my mother was also tough, but she never hit us. She was strict, and we never spoke back to her. And if we ever copped an attitude, she would give us that evil eye and throw her *chancla* (shoe) at us. It was like a damned boomerang. She never missed. (You **never, EVER** mess with Mom.)

I was told that my stepfather's family was hard and cold-blooded, showing few signs of affection or emotion. Their nature was just being hard workers and good providers, so that was the way we came to understand his custom and his life. I grew to dislike him over the years and later avoided him as much as possible. He was always very sarcastic and as mean as a junkyard dog. (Looking back, I probably should have bought him a big bone.)

The confrontations we had were usually either when nobody was home or late at night after he had been at the bars. He would try to engage me in a conversation that sometimes led to his provoking me, and then he tried using me as a punching bag. If I made any comments in response to his questions or gestures (like "What do you want?" or "Leave me alone."), he lunged at me and pushed or shoved me, and sometimes struck me—mostly with an open hand, but a few times with a closed fist. It's sad that, without fail, he'd always wake up the next morning and act like nothing had ever happened. I hated him for being this way and felt I did not deserve the verbal or physical abuse. I always thought he was a coward because he typically only grew hair on his chest when I was the only one around.

One late evening, he came home from work smelling like whiskey, as it was common at that time for him to go out drinking after work and then come home twisted. He was yelling at me and challenging me again, for no reason, about who knows what, standing at my bedroom door and gritting his teeth with a snarling face, trying to provoke me. I remember telling him to just go to bed. He lunged at me with a violent swing. Although I tried ducking, his fingernails ripped deep scratches across my face just beneath my right eye. I was young, and it was unheard of to take a swing back at your elders; besides, usually after he got in a few shots, that was enough for him and he'd wobble his intoxicated ass to bed so he could pass out for the night. The next morning, I told the kids at school that the bloody scratches on my face were caused by a cat that had attacked me. No one believed me because it wasn't the first time I had been seen with either scratches or fresh bruises. I guess my stepfather never realized or cared that he had humiliated me in front of all of my friends from school. Back in those days, we kept our lives private. No one ever said or reported anything about these types of situations; it was always swept under the carpet and people just looked the other way. I never told anyone about his drunken behavior and simply accepted his abuse silently.

My mother encountered her share of pain and run-ins with my stepfather, too. I remember one time when he got into a bad fight with her after he had, as usual, consumed too much alcohol. He busted what I believe was a glass over her head, causing her to bleed very badly all over herself. Those were wicked times, and I have never forgiven him for hurting my mother. She did eventually give him this final ultimatum: stop the crap or she would leave him for good. It's been well over thirty-five years now since he has touched my mother or me. Unfortunately, no cosmetic surgery can ever hide the emotional scars or the trail of bitter pain that he left behind.

My stepfather was a good provider and respectfully neat with his appearance. Reflecting back and trying to justify his actions and behavior, I know now that providing was clearly the only way he knew how to express his love. That **does not** excuse him, but he grew up in rough times, too. He was not a warm and fuzzy type of person, and it seems that he expressed his affections by always making sure there was food on the table, new shoes on our feet and a roof over our heads, for which I do respect him greatly. I will say he had very good work ethics, and I probably picked up much of my own personal work ethics from him. I don't think he ever really felt that he was being a terrible man. He believed in hard work and discipline, and maybe that was his way of trying to keep me off the streets. He did eventually find Christianity when I was in my teens, and it was a turning point in his life; it gave him a foundation that changed him and made him a better person.

Before he found religion, there were times when he was actually humane. For example, we would go fishing or dirt bike riding and he was just a regular guy, but not often enough. I guess he just did not know how to let himself express any affection. I admit that there were many times I both wanted and planned to either take him out or hurt him back so badly, but I realized that violence and revenge were not the right answer. Now, years later, he's just a cantankerous old man.

Much to my surprise, my mother is still married. She loves him very much and has a tremendous amount of respect for him for helping raise two children that were not his own. I also respect him for that and for being much more of a man than my old man (my biological father) had been. Anybody can make babies, but it's raising them and being there that counts. In my opinion, love is obviously very forgiving. Marriage is a lot of hard work and, unfortunately, the pay sucks, which is one reason I am single and focused on making a difference in the world. Someone said to me once, "If you want someone to love, buy a dog." In my case, I have a beautiful small white Manx cat named Blanca, although even she scratches and growls at me from time to time!

My mother had another child, my other baby sister, and she became our new reason for bigger dreams. We didn't want to expose her to the lifestyle we had suffered prior to her birth. My mother was desperate to get her three children out of East L.A.

She always supported my dreams and was always there to listen, just as she still is today. In fact, there isn't a day that goes by that I don't call back home to check on my family.

Growing up, my mother knew I never wanted to be a blue-collar worker. She watched me sit in front of that old, beat up black-and-white TV watching people who had nice cars, homes and jobs. She knew I dreamed of being one of those people because I always talked about it. After watching TV one afternoon, I promised her that one day I would buy her a new car and that I, too, would have nice clothes and all those things like the people on TV. She said to me, "No matter what you decide to do, simply be the best at it. If you are going to be a painter, then be the best painter. But, *mijo* (son), if you are ever going to have a business, then be the best in your business and do it with a *si se puede y con ganas* (yes, you can, and with guts) mentality."

My mother also told me that I should never hold my head down, feel sorry for myself, make lame excuses or point fingers because only children and cowards do this. I was taught to be responsible for my own actions, to respect others and myself, and to always share, even though we did not have much. Like most Latinos that wear their hearts on their sleeves, we gave the shirts off our backs and whatever little money we had to help anyone else who might have needed it.

One thing my mother always said that had great influence on me was that I was special—that I was the chosen one. I never understood what she was talking about at that young age. Now, I think it might mean that God gave me a gift, a second chance at life after the accident.

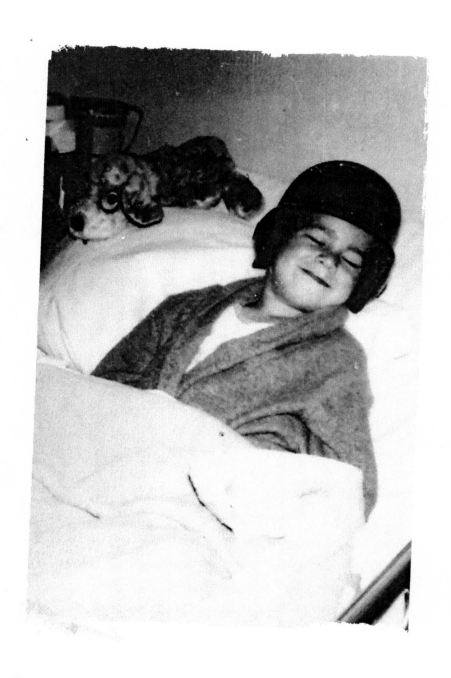

CHAPTER TWO

A Life-Changing Accident: I Became the Chosen One

When I was six years old, I was at a carnival with my family. I was exiting the octopus ride, and it abruptly started before I was completely off the ramp. It swung around and hit me solidly and directly on the front right side of my head, plunging me through a large crowd some fifty feet and busting my head wide open. A broken bone pushed through my skull, knocking me into a state of complete deliriousness. It was a catastrophe. I laid there on the ground bleeding to death with a compound fracture while dozens of people ran around me and screamed in total chaos. It was probably fifteen to twenty minutes before the ambulance arrived.

I was rushed to Beverly Hospital, which was not equipped or staffed to treat my severe head injury. My skull was fractured, and the bone that protruded through my smashed head left blood squirting out profusely. I was then immediately taken by the same ambulance to White Memorial Hospital, where a surgeon who had been brought in for someone else's brain surgery (by the chance of a miracle) rushed in to perform my emergency surgery.

The surgery lasted some seven and a half hours and required over two hundred stitches inside and out. Doctors also wired some bones back together inside my head and stabilized the setting and placement of bones.

My doctors told my mother, as kindly as they could, that because I was in critical condition, there was a chance I would not survive. They also said that if I did make it through the surgery, I may not know her. There was a huge possibility that I would not recover fully and be either mentally challenged or a vegetable. My mother fainted when hearing what the doctors had to say; she was in shock. The hospital chaplain stood over me, praying and reading from the bible while touching my bandaged head, giving me God's blessings. At the same time, there were some family members having private discussions about the possibility of preparing my funeral arrangements.

Numb with disbelief, my mother's faith in God would not allow her to believe anything other than that His hand would rest on my head to help heal me to full recovery. She stayed with me throughout the next forty-eight hours, sitting with me and praying silently, holding my hand and assuring me that I would be okay. Although I do not remember her talking to me as I lay in intensive care, tangled in a barrage of tubes and wires, my family told me that she never left my side. When I did wake up, still groggy and incoherent from the surgery, the first thing I said was, "Mom, where am I?" My mother embraced me. She was shaking and crying with tears of joy, thanking God for answering her prayers and saving her only son.

Nobody expected that moment except my mother. I'm sure that her undying love and care during those long, dreadful two days, and her faith in God were a huge part of why I survived. I literally went from looking death in the face to one step short of being resurrected and fighting my way back so I can now tell you the details of my survival and of God's plans for my destiny.

Although the doctors continued to grimly warn my mother of my chances for a full recovery, they continued to perform many tests because my head was so damaged and my brain so swollen and bruised. From what we were told by the surgeon as he shook his head in disbelief, it was a one in a million chance that I recovered from the trauma at all.

My mother continued to work while I remained in the hospital, hooked up to medical monitors and fighting to recover. She worked the night shift and then came to the hospital in the morning and stayed there all day. Occasionally, she caught a few winks sitting up on the chair, but she mostly spent the day talking with me or just tightly holding my hand before going back to work—a routine she followed for six straight weeks. She was certainly exhausted from no real sleep or even the luxury of a real bed. But the one thing I remember clearly from my recovery in the hospital was my mother's beautiful smile and her assuring me, time and time again, not to worry—that everything was going to be okay.

My grandparents watched my little sister during this time, but my mother would wash and change at the hospital and go to and from work, trying to leave me alone only to go to work and then return to the side of my hospital bed.

I did lose a fair amount of weight from being hooked up to the IV and eating small portions of hospital food. I hated being in the hospital, and I missed my family.

Following dozens of physical therapy sessions, the doctors finally said I no longer needed to stay in the hospital. So, after eight long weeks, I was released to go home in a wheelchair to be with my family again, which was strange because I had limited and deteriorated motor skills. It was several weeks later before I was fully able to get my balance again and stand on solid ground. I was able to speak and get around, but it was a slow process, and I made improvements every day.

I remember wanting to be back to my normal self and pushing myself hard, which was probably why I was making positive progress. I was very hyper for several months following the accident; the doctors explained to my mom that I was moving faster inside my head than I was moving outside, causing me to pace a lot and be very fidgety—almost like a nervous reaction. I underwent weekly X-rays, CAT scans, and mental evaluations during my recovery. It took about three years to finally get me to the place where I leveled off to a normal pace. My mother told me that my grandfather would cry at night, worried that I would never be normal again.

Shortly after I was released from the hospital, I was sent to a handicapped school for the physically disabled and mentally challenged. My motor skills needed to be rehabilitated, and I had to basically relearn everything from scratch. My head had gone under complete reconstructive surgery and was like an egg yolk that needed to be protected, which is why I was medically required to wear a football helmet (without the mask) while I underwent continued care and made my recovery. The special school was filled with severely disabled and deformed children, missing arms or legs, mentally challenged and handicapped. I was subjected to an environment unlike anything I had ever seen or even known existed at that age. They mixed all of us children together for meals and on the playground (huge mistake!), and I remember feeling terrified, screaming and pleading with everyone to let me go home. Every day was a repeat performance of the same living nightmare.

I had to wait three long, grueling years before I could take off that helmet, which I hated, but I wore it everywhere every day. I finally got to go back to a public school, but the terrible memories of the things I saw in that rehabilitation school have stayed with me. In fact, nightmares of my experiences there still haunt me to this day; my memories of handicapped and awkward children remind me of the sense of helplessness I felt while there. I can't forget the sight of watching deformed children trying to eat as food fell out of their mouths while nurses tried assisting them, nor can I forget the sounds made by some children who could not properly speak. I still question if the school staff was properly trained or medically qualified to provide the type of care those children needed.

One recurring nightmare that I still have is of a young girl lying on a bed in a full-body metal brace facing the door. As I look into the room, I see her throwing up—the vomit running down the side of the bed, dripping to the floor as she lays there gagging with her face in the mess. No one comes to clean her up for hours. I go back to look and see she is still lying there in her own vomit. It was absolutely heartbreaking. My three years there was nothing less than a horrific experience.

I was warned after my accident about my chances of survival and made aware that I would probably never live a normal life, playing sports like most other kids, yet I went on to do so and functioned no less than anyone else did. In fact, I not only survived, but I thrived. I was an exceptional athlete, playing football, basketball, baseball and racquetball. I was remarkably normal, and no one ever knew, going forward, about the accident once I fell back into the normal routine of living.

But looking back, I remember all the people that told my mother that I would likely never be able to walk, talk, read or write, and how she **NEVER** listened to them. Instead she took me to doctor after doctor after doctor pushing me beyond human endurance, and when I'd fall she'd pick me up and push me some more.

Finally the day came when I walked out the front gates of that school, tall, strong, and on my own. I remember my mother crying with tears streaming down her face. That day proved to me that happiness was not about pleasure. Happiness was about Victory! (We had done what they said could not be done).

CHAPTER THREE

Gang Life: My Rebel Years in East L.A.

When my mother remarried and later had my second little sister, Regina, we moved to Orange County, California, where we purchased a small home in a better neighborhood and began a new life. We moved because my mother did not want to bring up my new baby sister (known affectionately as "the brat") in the same depressing and miserable environment that we had grown up in, and she was determined to give all of us a better life.

I started junior high there and attended for two years, with another two and a half in high school, before dropping out. My personal life at home was again difficult, because my stepfather remained mean and very hard to get along with. I wasn't allowed many opportunities to go out and socialize like most of the kids I went to school with.

Still, despite my stepfather's stringency, there were ways of getting by him. I would sneak out of the house after he'd passed out drunk or just lie to get out and socialize. Since my stepfather never attended any of my school functions or sports events, I would simply say that I had a game and instead go with some friends to a party or just go hang out at somebody's house having a few drinks. It was an embarrassing secret that I kept from my friends at school—that I was literally a prisoner in my own home.

Part-time jobs were my only real liberty or release from being home, because those were the only times he wouldn't bother me. I always worked, even as a small kid. I flipped pizzas for $1.00 an hour and worked at the car wash on Saturdays and Sundays for $1.83 an hour. I mowed lawns, painted, and worked at McDonald's, learning customer service with a smile, and bussed plenty of restaurant tables. I delivered papers, worked as a janitor (cleaning more than my fair share of toilets), tried working as a mechanic and, of course, held several manual labor factory jobs.

The gang situation, unfortunately, was a necessary evil. If you did not belong to a gang or hang around with those guys, you were open prey to everyone. But if other kids knew you had taken a "side" and you didn't wander off alone, they would not mess with you most of the time. Being with the homeboys was simply a way to have someone cover your back while on the streets. If I had to do it all over again, I sure as hell would not be looking for love in all the wrong places.

As a small child growing up, we lived around some pretty bad people, and I learned quickly that I had to be tough to survive. Back then, I fought to protect myself, because it was either fight back or face the possibility of being hurt severely. Like almost everyone, I ran around with guys who were in a gang, so other gangs would try to catch me away from the group and pick me off—usually several guys against me. If someone did not like the way I looked, or dressed, or if I was messing with the wrong girl or on the wrong side of town, things got ugly. I felt pressured to continually look over my shoulder, knowing there was always the possibility that someone was out to get me.

I was walking home from junior high school when five Latino "gang-bangers," all about my age, jumped out from beside a house and surrounded me, wanting my jacket. I fought back with desperation, and popped a couple of these guys hard in the face, but I was attacked and tackled to the ground. One of the guys pulled a knife and stuck me in the thigh, while the others punched and kicked me. It seemed like the fight lasted for hours. I thought they were cowards because they all ran off like a bunch of little girls, screaming the name of their gang once they got my jacket.

Fortunately, the knife wound was not deep and I was able to limp a few blocks over to a friend's house and clean and bandage it myself. I did not want to have to explain anything to the police, or, especially to my mother. I tried keeping this very dark side of my life away from most of my family—my uncle was probably the only one who knew the score, the real deal about the drugs and some of my shady activities. The funny part about that fight was that the jacket was full of holes and didn't fit me anyway. (Idiots!)

Gangs had territories, which is pretty dumb when you think about it: a bunch of guys running around protecting what we considered "our turf." While I was in high school, I was caught fooling around with a girl from the wrong side of the tracks. Some gang members from her side of town saw me kissing her and decided to come after me. One late afternoon when I was walking away from the high school campus, four Chicano homeboys *(vatos locos)* from the barrio across the tracks drove by in a Chevy low-rider, pulled out a rifle and started shooting at me. I remember my adrenaline was pumping as I ran like hell in a zigzag pattern to dodge the bullets. They missed, and I obviously stopped seeing the girl—not because I was afraid, but because I was, like my grandfather used to say, *"poco loco, pero no pendejo"* (a little crazy, but not stupid!).

I have been knifed, shot at and beat up more times than I care to discuss, but I gave back more than my fair share as well. Do you know why nobody wants to fight a Latino? It's because we don't give up! I've been black and blue a few times, but I was never afraid to fight. My fights, however, were **never** because I wanted to be malicious or hurt anyone. I always fought to protect myself and shamefully, carrying guns and knives was the way things worked back then. Plenty of times I was involved in cir-cumstances that could have very easily found me six feet under. There was one time when I made a deal to steal some cars with a guy who was connected—a *mafioso*—and the deal went bad. Now, these guys that I was playing with were not junior varsity. They played for keeps. In fact, my uncle, who had covered my back more than once, had to step in with his contacts and threaten these guys or they would have otherwise tried having me dusted, and my life would have been history. I will have to live with myself forever, painfully regretting all of the terrible things I have done in my past.

It doesn't matter if you're careful or not, it all eventually catches up with you. You might not get caught, but you still have to live with what you've done, and guilt is a heavy burden.

Having lived through the violence and the confrontations on the street, I can tell you that gangbanging and violence is not a lifestyle. It is a "death-style." Being involved with gangs in my teens up until I turned twenty-one was definitely not one of the better choices I made in my life, nor one of which I am proud.

I worked from a very young age doing chores for people to make extra money for the family. In eleventh grade, I dropped out of school and got a job, following the path of most Latinos and underprivileged families at that time who wanted to put bread on the table. This is a vicious cycle that has been occurring in our culture for generations. About that time, I moved in with my aunt and uncle (my godparents) for a few months because I could no longer live with my stepfather. When I moved in with them, I actually experienced real freedom. My aunt and uncle were good, genuine people. My aunt, who was married to my mother's brother, was a very attractive, classy and intelligent woman who talked with me about her banking career. She really got me thinking about money and business, as she and my uncle had a nice home, nice cars and a wonderful lifestyle. Looking back at those conversations about finances, I know that it was more than just TV; it was my aunt—my godmother—God rest her soul, who influenced me in my thoughts about diversity and success.

After I quit school, I began working as many hours as I could, probably twelve hours every day, six, sometimes seven days a week. In my off time, I ran with a bunch of guys who only wanted to drink and party, our normal week-to-week activity. I was out drinking and chasing girls just about every chance I got. I also sold and smoked marijuana and, shamefully enough, smoked some angel dust (PCP), took tabs of acid, and snorted and sold cocaine. (It's scary, looking back and realizing how terribly close I came to ruining my life.)

My first car was a hand-me-down 1968 VW Bug. It was old and beat up, and the seats were torn to hell. The Bug was a primer gray with severely worn tires, and it ran like it was on its last leg. I worked the graveyard shift at a bottle factory stacking boxes off the conveyor onto palettes and saved my money for a newly rebuilt engine, new tires with Porsche rims, and all new insides. Then I had it painted a beautiful pearl white and installed a smokin' stereo system. My Bug was so clean that I used to run around from time to time with a car club back in the late 70s called the California Cruisers.

My buddies and I would cruise to Whittier Boulevard on Friday or Saturday nights and then drive up and down the strip drinking beer, cruising for girls and smoking a joint while listening to oldies but goodies like "All My Friends Know the Low Rider" and "You're My Angel, Baby."

Even before I fixed up my Bug, when it still looked as crappy as it did, I still had the guts to ask girls to go out with me, in hopes that my good looks, blue eyes and charming personality— rather than the car—would be the hook. I had plenty of dates, even with my Herbie! Those were simple times. Dates usually consisted of getting a bottle of Boone's Farm wine and going to a garage party, getting drunk and fooling around. There wasn't a lot of extra money, but we went to dances or a drive-in movie every once in a while. I asked the girls to go with me to simple places and, before I had fixed up the car, always got the same disgusted look once they got into the Bug—it's actually quite funny now because they went anyway.

In the late 70s and early 80s, I had a fake ID. It was about the time *Saturday Night Fever* came out, and I often dressed up in my Angel Flight suit with my platform shoes and polyester shirt, and hit the clubs with my buddies, dancing to disco music all night long. Back then, I believed the people I ran with were so cool, and I thought I was, too. Those were memorable times, full of encounters with girls. We often took them to my friend's house following a late night of abusive drinking, smoking pot, partying and getting completely stoned out of our minds. We were living *la vida loca* (the crazy life). Sex back then was simply very casual, and we had no concerns about diseases—just being wild and free, loving and enjoying every minute of it.

I have always loved women immensely, and believe me, I still do. There have been so many women in my life that I can't honestly say how many or tell you all of their names. Truth be told, one of the things that probably saved me from the drugs and alcohol (besides my mother) was my love and passion for women. If I have any other addiction than for success in life, it is my love and desire for the different fruits of passion.

True love has hit me only once in my life. I'm fifty years young now, and I realize that even though I have been with women from so many different parts of the world, only one has truly touched my soul. She remains a precious memory locked up deep inside my heart—protected as the one true love of my life. There isn't a day that goes by that I don't regret the fact that I let someone so special slip right through my fingers. She was absolutely beautiful, both inside and out. I still miss the smell of her sweet perfume, her gentle touch, her kiss and her warm, soft, tender body. Hell, just the thought of her still gets me excited. My baby girl was so fine I would have drunk her bath water. She was such a hot-blooded Latina, she'd make any man want to speak Spanish. If there were only a way to just turn back the hands of time, I could tell her how much I still love her, and I would be with her today.

I did date occasionally growing up, but never really had any long-term relationships. Let's be honest: it takes a lot of money to afford a steady girlfriend! Still, I was with girls on a regular basis when I managed to sneak away from the warden (my step-father) and have some private encounters at some of the girls' houses or at the homes of some of my buddies.

Now I just enjoy casual dating with no strings and no obligation to call or send flowers. Don't get me wrong; I love women, romance and passion more today than ever, and my sexual drive, too, is much stronger than ever before. Remember, I am a Latino! But for me, it's an issue of keeping my priorities straight. I own my own business, and I am now writing books to fulfill my dream of reaching out and making a global offering to all races in hopes of helping people understand that we are not a carbon copy, but an original; each of us is our own masterpiece.

Do I ever want to settle down? That's a great question and, without contradicting myself, the answer is "I don't know." I believe that I am honest with myself, and because of all I have seen and been exposed to, I do not know if I can buy into the fact that either men or women are absolutely honest with each other anymore. People today simply have too many choices, but I do remain optimistic to the possibilities. I will keep my options wide open in the hope that I will know what it's like to be loved and to love again. (Women are definitely, without question, one of life's most precious gifts.)

Back when I was seventeen years old, my estranged uncle (my father's younger brother), who was a Catholic priest, called to tell me that my father had died. I do not know how he got my telephone number, and I never asked. We had no real relationship with my father's side of the family other than that they knew about us and we knew about them. We tried several times over the years to contact my grandmother and uncle, but they rarely responded or showed any interest in getting together with my sister or me. Sure as hell didn't say much about them practicing their Catholic beliefs.

When my uncle called to tell me that my father had died, he said he felt that I should be the one to go and get his personal belongings from where he had lived. I was curious and interested to find out who my real father was and what he was all about, and I knew, without question, that this would be my only, and last chance to make these discoveries for myself.

I had never seen a crack-house or halfway house before, let alone ever been on Skid Row, nor had I ever been exposed to such an extreme group of derelicts as the ones I found where my father was living. This was a pretty hardcore group, like something out of a bad movie. I was in disbelief as the pimps, prostitutes, bums, drunks and drug addicts asked me for money as I slowly walked through the flickering lights of the stale-smelling hallway toward the room where my father had apparently lived for two years prior to his death.

The clerk at the front desk provided me a key because I had a copy of the hospital paperwork showing that he had died. When I finally made it to my father's room, I unlocked the door and stood there quietly looking at the damp, smelly, dirty and very tiny one-room dump with nothing but a couple of empty bottles of booze in the trashcan. At that very moment, I could not help but feel sorry for my mother. It was like déjà vu, because this was exactly how he had left us fourteen years earlier when I was just a toddler.

As I stood there alone in the dark room, sad and disgusted, collecting my thoughts and trying to remotely understand just who this man had really been, a woman suddenly walked in wearing a torn and dirty blue robe. A skinny white woman who was probably in her late twenties, she reeked of urine and alcohol and was obviously on some sort of drug. She stood there with glazed eyes, somewhat off-balance, and then opened her robe and exposed her naked self, asking me if I wanted to have sex or get a blowjob for ten dollars. I grabbed the plastic crucifix that was hanging on the headboard of the small dirty bed that my father had slept on and got out of the building as quickly as possible.

I kept that crucifix and the one-dollar bill that he had on him when he died until I began the process of writing this book. After holding on to these possessions for almost thirty years, I recently gave them to my mother. She put my name and my sister's name on the dollar and put it away with the crucifix somewhere safe. My mother cried when I gave these things to her and commented that he could have been so much more if it weren't for the drugs and alcohol. But it goes to prove that if you are going to play with the devil, you're going to get burned. I know several people, both men and women, who have told me they have it all under control. Sure! (It's called denial.) Many of these same people have lost everything they ever worked for: their houses, cars, jobs and, sadly enough, even their families—and for what? Don't be a fool; you can't control drugs or alcohol. They will always, no matter what, take control of you. (If you need help—GET HELP!)

Following my father's death, I continued working nights at the bottle factory and moved back in with my grandparents and the uncle who was taking care of them in East L.A. Our grandparents were not very healthy and did not work. My uncle is a very good, honest and decent man who literally sacrificed his own personal life to take care of my grandparents—his parents—throughout their entire lives. Although my grandparents have passed away, my uncle is very close to me even today, and we care for one another as actual brothers.

My grandfather and I had a very special bond that is difficult to explain, but he loved me like his own son. My grandparents did not have much to offer financially, but they had big hearts just like my mother, which is probably why I am a soft touch when it comes right down to it. When I was twenty, my grandfather began talking with me about getting out of L.A. and starting a new life somewhere else. He was not crazy at all about my friends and the boozing, along with the various other unspoken activities with which I was involved. He was angry with me because I was just running my life in circles like a dog chasing its tail. He told me that I had an opportunity to be anything I wanted to be in life and that he wanted more for me. He was afraid that if I stayed in the old neighborhoods, I would end up in jail or dead; and even in the best-case scenario, I would be working in a dead-end factory job.

My grandfather cried while he shared with me his regrets about not making more out his own life, and although he loved his family with all his heart, he wished he would have traveled and maybe taken the time and made the effort to open a business. He said that one day I would be old, and he did not want me to be like a lot of older people sitting in a barroom, having a drink and saying, "I wish I would have..." or "I wonder what would have happened if..." He said that although I was Latino/Mexican, people would look at me differently because of my light skin and blue eyes and accept me in the real world. At the time, I had no clue what he was talking about, but later in my life, it all came together and made perfect sense.

He insisted on always speaking to me in Spanish, telling me that it would be an important part of my future. Again, I had no clue, but his golden wisdom proved to be a huge benefit to me socially, as well as a very big part of my business world. (Thanks, Grandpa, for making me listen!) I knew that his advice and the things he shared with me came from his personal regrets, hardships and experiences.

When I turned twenty-one, he pulled me aside again and said to me, "Wake up! Life will pass you by in the blink of an eye. You have to have *ganas* (guts), desire, drive and passion if you are going to be somebody." He continued, "I bet that if you go away and come back in ten years, these guys you are running around with now will still be right here doing the same thing, if they're even alive at all." He told me he believed in me and wanted me to get my shit together—and not just for him or my family, but for myself. I thought back to how I had seen my father's life end four years earlier. As I recalled those final moments, when we buried the man that fathered me, it suddenly became crystal clear that my grandfather was absolutely right—I needed to get out of L.A. If I was going to climb the ladder of life in the business world that I had always talked about, my best chance was to get a fresh start somewhere new. It was then that I decided to join the U.S. Army, see the world and "be all that I could be/Army strong." My only problem was that I needed to get my GED to be accepted into the armed forces.

I vigorously pursued taking evening classes before going to work each night. The hours were hell, because I was pulling double graveyard shifts and going to school early evenings totally zoned out, but in the end, after several months, I received certificates for both my GED and my high school equivalency.

My mother was happy for me when I told her that I had joined the military and was going to Europe on my first assignment. Not a bad way to travel for a poor Latino boy from East L.A. The deal I made with my grandfather and mother was that I would give the Army my best shot and do everything possible to benefit from the opportunity in front of me. I also promised that I would make them proud, not let them down, and would always send postcards and call from all of the places I visited so that they could share in my experiences as if they were there seeing it for themselves.

I did not want to end up like my real father, and I had no mixed emotions or fears about leaving. I believed in my heart that this was the best thing to do and that it was a real, honest opportunity for me to get the hell out of the barrio. Considering that either crime, drugs, or death were quite likely my alternatives, I can say unquestionably that I made the right decision.

CHAPTER FOUR

The Military: No Racism, Everybody's Green

In 1983, following many conversations with my grandfather, I decided that it was time for me to go and make a real life for myself. I gave a lot of thought to his bet that I could leave and come back in ten years and see the same guys I was hanging around with still here doing the exact same things—if they were even still alive.

In July 1983, I swore into the U.S. Army and left for boot camp at Fort Sill, Oklahoma, with several hundred young men from all over the United States. It was initially very difficult, mixing all of our complex personalities, probably because of our immaturity and a need to prove we were tougher than each other (a guy thing).

The fact that we trained all day and were confined at night to a barracks (and literally together 24/7 for the entire twelve weeks) created more of a survival-of-the-fittest mentality. Some guys were simply trying to impose their will and position themselves as the leaders of the group, so they used physical violence to intimidate one another. A few recruits requested to be released because of their fear, and a few others got busted up pretty badly and were actually released for medical reasons. Back in those days, nobody ever said anything about this type of behavior, at least as I understood it while I was there. I never asked any questions. I just figured it was considered acceptable and maybe even part of the training.

As I recall, I had at least three fights while in boot camp because some of the guys challenged me to be a follower and concede that there was going to be only one *el mas macho* (the toughest guy). This was the only time in my seven-plus years in the military service that I was in a position of opposition with my fellow soldiers. But after about two or three weeks, no one dude sat on top as the leader—we just all started to become more of a group rather than individuals on opposing sides. I have to believe that the drill instructors allowed us to figure this out on our own, at least initially. I did miss my family and, but for a brief moment, even started to second-guess myself about being there. But I had given my grandfather and mother my word.

I remember getting into some rather rough scraps with a few of the guys. I actually busted up my right hand pretty good in one of the fistfights and never told anyone (until now). Another fight got so out of hand that a guy pulled a knife and tried to stab me, and I became so enraged that I reached for a soda bottle and busted it across his forehead. I then grabbed a chair and hit him over the top of his head, knocking him to the ground and leaving him a little bit bloody and battered. I believe it was a simple matter of a bunch of guys trying to survive under a different kind of regime.

Once things leveled off with everyone, we began to focus on training, working together and developing some harmony. It was then that we really began to move in the same direction and assert ourselves. The training was physically demanding every day in blistering, hundred degree plus temperatures, but it felt like we had finally begun to accomplish the objectives for which we were there in the first place.

We were up every morning before the crack of dawn. The drill instructors would burst into the barracks, screaming right up in our faces to get our asses out of our bunks and onto the training field. We would run around in pandemonium, each of us knocking into one another, falling all over ourselves and trying to get dressed and fight our way out the door. Finally, there we were, young men lined up, row after row, going through the physical fitness training and refusing to quit. We ran mile after mile, dripping in sweat, with the smell of stifling body odor all around us. I had probably lost a good fifteen pounds during boot camp, but I was a lean, mean, fighting machine.

During the rifle, machine gun, grenade and rocket launcher training, as well as through rigorous survival training sessions, everyone finally started pulling together and providing support and assistance if someone was not mustarding up to the tasks.

Looking back now, some twenty-one years later, I realize that the Army taught me that there is no such thing as going halfway, just as there is no such thing as being a little bit pregnant—you're either pregnant or you're not. The Army taught me that you are either in or out—there was no middle ground. (It's the will of the man that makes the skill of the man.)

Following my completion of boot camp training, I was assigned to a small base overseas just outside of Nuremburg, Germany. I remember thinking, *I wonder if they have Mexican food there?* I spent over two years in Europe, working and training with a tactical operations unit directly supporting the artillery soldiers in the field. I worked for a lieutenant colonel who spent a lot of time schooling me on the finer points of strategic planning and warfare. While in Europe, I had some of the best beer in the world and got a chance to participate in the authentic Oktoberfest, enjoying pilsner beer, weiss beer and, of course, the beautiful German Fräuleins (women).

After completing my overseas assignment, I was transferred stateside to the 1st Cavalry Division in Fort Hood, Texas, where I became interested in pursuing air assault and airborne military occupational advancements. I was then reassigned to Ft. Bragg, North Carolina, and served in a psychological operations unit. Eventually, I made my way through Fort Benning, Georgia, with the Ranger battalions, and then went back to Fort Bragg, where

I ultimately ended up being part of spearheading the reactivation of a Special Forces unit. Proudly wearing a green beret, I was assigned to various classified duties and jumped out of more airplanes and helicopters than I can remember.

During my many memorable tours of duty, I had the opportunity to advance in rank. In 1987, I was promoted as a non-commissioned officer. The creed of a non-commissioned officer is to be a leader of soldiers; he is a member of a time-honored corps known as "the backbone of the Army." I am proud of the corps of non-commissioned officers and conducted myself at all times in a manner that brought credit upon the corps, military service and my country. That rank brought an obligation to lead and command groups of men, and I was responsible for their personal welfare, well-being and professional training in their occupational specialty. It was my duty to ensure that each of them was more than proficient with weapons, explosives and bio-chemical warfare. It was also my job to make sure that they were physically and mentally able to execute if given the call to serve our country.

The things I was trained to do stayed with me and have become core values and principles that I live by each and every day. Sacrifices I made while in the military were, in my opinion, a labor of love for my country.

It was lonely being so far away from home, especially while overseas because I was unable to share in holidays, birthdays and special events. Although I kept my promises to call and send postcards every week, if possible, so that my family could share in my experiences, it was nonetheless difficult having to travel down all those dark, lonely highways.

As a young man serving his country several thousand miles from home, I learned that the people I shared my tours of duty with were the closest thing I had to family while I was away. The Army is where I learned the true meaning of "Band of Brothers."

We joked and smoked, meaning when it was time to play, we played hard, but when it was time to work, we got down to business and took our jobs and responsibilities seriously. While I was in the military, the normal evening activity was hanging out at the NCO club talking shit and drinking until everyone passed out. It was not very different from being back home except that we were not all trying to kill each other. There was a code that we lived by: a code of honor, respect, integrity, determination and discipline. Unless you have served in the armed forces, it's probably a little hard to comprehend what our code of ethics really meant. Sure, there are many good people who have not served in the military. But life looks different when you put your country first and yourself second. It takes on a completely new perspective because there is a price being paid every day by our military who bears that cross with honor so we can live in the world as we know it—the land of the free.

The military was (and is) all about systems and procedures. If you followed the rules, the system would work for you. If you bucked the system, you were guaranteed to fail. Adhering to proper protocol and following the chain of command were basic rules to abide by. Many of my current senses and gut feelings largely stem from what I learned and how I was trained during those years. My instincts became cat-like; I found the keen ability to make snap decisions. Just as in life, the details in the military are the difference between them killing you or you killing them. Facts be told, when given the order, we did our jobs or people died—literally. It's important to remember that the devil is in the details.

I encountered thousands of people, both men and women, in my travels during tours of duty, and it was an unspoken rule that we looked after one another. It was like being in one big badass gang. Regardless of race or economic background, we were all the same—Army green. Having the opportunity to work with large groups of people who aligned themselves to share in achieving common goals and objectives was actually a very rewarding and gratifying experience that taught me skills and principles that later helped me in business.

The Army helps build character and helps you learn about honor and dedication for yourself, your peers and your country. The word "commitment" sticks with me when I think about the military. I learned a lot about standing tall, facing my fears and giving my all unconditionally, not just for myself, but also for the men and women who served with me. Through some really unexplainable chains of events and emotions, I find myself holding onto the experiences shared with these people as some of my most memorable and valuable lessons. In 1983, I took the oath as follows: "I, Robert Jess Renteria Jr., do solemnly swear (or affirm) that I will support and defend the constitution of the United States against all enemies, foreign and domestic; and I will bear true faith and allegiance to the same; and that I will obey the orders of the President of the United States and the orders of the officers appointed over me, according to the regulations and the Uniform Code of Military Justice, so help me God."

I am forever grateful to my grandfather and the U.S. Army for pushing me, and grateful to the thousands of men and women in the military who shared with me a cohesive effort in coming together as one fierce force! "United we stand, divided we fall." The military gave me the ability to make sound decisions, and I felt that—for me, at least—pushing the envelope was going to be better than licking it. You can either follow the crowd or venture out on the edge. (The road you choose will ultimately decide your destiny.)

The fundamental building blocks of the Army and my experiences as I worked my way through the ranks to become a noncommissioned officer gave me the business perspective I needed to be confident enough in myself to leap back into the real world and make another run at my civilian life. This time,I was prepared and equipped to stand up and not just be a man, but a better man and a leader instead of just another loser standing on street corners crying in his beer, hanging out every night getting annihilated, doing drugs, howling at the moon and pissing his life away.

Through my tours of duty and assignments, I had been a part of something important. I learned what "same mud, same blood" meant, and I was proud to have had the opportunity to serve and protect the American people. The Army gives you a chance to be a part of something bigger than you are. As an American Soldier, seeing our flag flying high was special for me, and I was honored to share in the camaraderie and patriotism of our country. I would definitely recommend the military to all young men and women who are trying to find their way prior to taking their leap into adulthood. The military both changed and, very likely, saved my life. I am proud to be a Mexican, born and raised in the USA.

CHAPTER FIVE

Fire in My Belly: The Climb to Corporate America

Following my honorable discharge from the military in late September of 1990 and a brief stay back in California, I decided I needed to move, get a fresh start and begin yet another chapter in my life. My grandfather was right about me going away and coming home to find the same crowd I had previously run around with still doing the same things as they were when I left. The only real difference now was that six of these so-called friends had graduated their substance abuse to heroin, cocaine and drug dealing. Two of them got blasted and lost their lives to drugs and gang violence, and one is serving twenty-years-to-life, handcuffed and shackled in a cold world surrounded by metal bars, wearing a yellow jump suit, with nothing more to look forward to than three "hots" and a cot, being told how to walk, talk, when to eat and when to sleep. (My grandfather always said, *"Dime quien son tus amigos, y te digo quien eres."* (Show me your friends and I'll tell you who you are.) In life, you have to make sure that you are willing to live with the choices you make.

I had run into a few of the old so-called friends at a nightclub, and they actually called me a punk and a sell-out. I guess they were pissed off that I did not choose to be part of their lives anymore. Imagine that (proves that misery loves company). My feelings about these guys now were disgust, sorrow and pity. I realized by just looking at them that there was no way that I was going to lose hope or sight of my dreams and allow myself to be pulled back into the proverbial gutter that I had worked so hard to pull myself out of just seven and a half years prior. I wish that I could say that my time and experiences in the military might have been a positive influence on some of these guys, but in the end, you cannot help someone who doesn't want to be helped. On the other hand, if you see someone—anyone—who wants to change, by all means, please, reach out and help pull them out and take them with you. Everyone deserves a chance. Everyone!

I had a friend in Chicago, actually more of an acquaintance, who had told me to call him if I ever needed to get away, so I made the call and asked if I could come to Chicago and stay with him while I looked for a job. He agreed. I packed my duffle bag, put my last two hundred dollars cash in my pocket, and boarded a plane with a ticket that my family had pitched in to buy. As the airplane taxied on the runway, I sensed that the wheels of fate had taken a turn, and I wasn't going back.

I stayed with my friend in his very small suburban Chicago apartment, sleeping at night on the living room floor and spending my days searching through local papers trying to find a job. I was eager to get going in any direction just so that I could jump-start my life again. I did not want to be a burden to my friend, but I had no money to contribute to the rent or anything else. I was very frugal with the money I had, using it only to buy food for myself. I ate mostly at Arby's because they offered a special of five sandwiches for five dollars. Things were tight when I first arrived, and I literally tried to spread those sandwiches out for most of the week by eating only one sandwich per day and drinking lots of water. I was also quite far behind in paying my maxed out credit card debts, and in early 1991, because I had no money, I was left with no other alternative but to file bankruptcy.

After almost six weeks of trying to find a job, my friend told me that there was a possible opening at the company where he worked, so I had the opportunity for an interview with the owner. The company was a commercial laundry sales and distribution organization. On the day of my big interview, I put on my best "Sunday go-to-meeting" duds and drove to work with my friend.

He showed me around, and then I finally sat down for the big moment. The owner looked to be a pleasant man who asked me about my background and told me about his company. He said they needed a right-hand to the construction supervisor and the Vice President.

Because I had no real business experience and no history of longevity at any real job other than the military, he passed on hiring me but wished me well. I paused for a moment and he asked me if I was okay. I sternly looked at him and said, "Sir, I ask you to please reconsider!"

"What do you mean?" he asked. I told him that I was fluent in Spanish and that I was a hard worker. I told him that I could see he had a big, beautiful business and that he obviously took a lot of pride in his company. I assured him that if he gave me a chance, he would not regret the decision. I promised to show my worth and told him that if he was not happy with my performance after only three months, I would leave on my own. I explained a bit about my culture and told him that my family members were honest, hardworking people who took a lot of pride in our work. Finally, I again assured him that hiring me would be a good decision for him and his company because I would protect his company as if it were my own, working seven days a week if needed to get the job done. I also told him I would never steal from him.

He looked at me a bit puzzled, put his hand on the side of his face, tipped his glasses and frowned, looking down at the conference room table. Then just as suddenly, he got up from the table, asked me to give him a minute and walked out. The door closed behind him, leaving me alone in the conference room. Those few minutes seemed like hours as I sat there perspiring and looking at the pictures on the walls, secretly wondering if he was calling the police to have me removed from the property. He came back into the room, sat down and grinned as he looked at me from across the table. "Let's discuss compensation," he said. I had never been in a negotiation or even a real interview, but I nervously explained what I was looking for in terms of salary. I told him that since the job likely required a lot of driving, I would need a company vehicle. After a discussion that lasted about an hour, he put his hand out and said, "Welcome aboard!"

As I left the conference room and crossed the showroom floor to my friend's office, I remember trying to keep a straight face, knowing that my new journey was beginning! Oh, and I did get a salary (more than comparable to what I was making in the military), expenses and a new company car. Just in time, too, because I was flat broke!

Now that I had a job, I made it a point every day to be the first person to show up. I was told that the owner was always there at 6:30 in the morning to open up, so on my first day, I was there at 6:15, ready and waiting to go to work. When he saw me there as he arrived, his mouth dropped.

"What are you doing here so early?" he asked.

"I told you I was going to protect the company as if it were my own and that I would work hard for you. I am here to go to work!"

He smiled, shook his head and let me in. I went to my small office and began to get organized so that when the Vice President and the construction supervisor showed up, I would be ready to go.

The first few months, I stuck close to both of them, asking many questions and acting like a fly on the wall, listening very carefully to what they discussed and observing how things got done.

Obviously, I did not know anything about the commercial coin laundry industry in the beginning. I was listening and taking everything in, much like a student going to college and working for a degree. It was important for me to gather as much knowledge as possible from these guys because of their many years of experience in the industry. I believed that the acquired knowledge, combined with my desire to be somebody, would be my strength and my power in the years to come. The industry was about site locations—either owning the land or renting spaces to put in a new laundromat (coin operated washers and dryers), as well as selling equipment to existing laundry owners who were adding new machines to expand or replacing old machines with new ones. The business was not difficult to understand; I merely needed to get my arms around all the details.

We also trained laundry owners to service their equipment and helped with marketing plans and ongoing business consulting. I piggybacked my mentors, following them around and listening until I felt that I had a solid grasp of the business so that I could talk to customers and prospects on my own. I learned about brokerage (buying and selling laundries), got a better feel for developing a business plan when purchasing a business, and gained an understanding of how the demographics would best cater to a successful laundry location. I watched those guys work with contractors, set up schedules, read blueprints, design a floor plan and work with various architects. Initially, selling washers and dryers did not appeal to me because I felt that salesmen were fast-talking, shady people. I'm not certain, but I suspect someone led me to believe while I was growing up that you can't trust salespeople or lawyers.

The friend I lived with, who had gotten me the interview, had a fall-out with management and was fired. He left Chicago and moved away—I never found out where he went, as we never communicated again after he left Illinois. I was not bitter about him leaving, nor was he with me. The owner told me that he did not want my friend's leaving to affect me staying because everyone liked me and appreciated my work ethics and my "can and will do" attitude toward whatever it took to get the job done.

So there I was, after about ten months in the game, living alone in Chicago with no friends or family, but a new job. I had to make a decision to stay on track with my goals and to focus on making a success of myself. My friend's small one-bedroom apartment where I once slept on the floor was now mine, but it was empty because he took all of his belongings when he left. I literally had an empty apartment with nothing to my name except my job and whatever other little bits of clothing I had hanging in my closet. Even so, I did not intend to go back to my former life, even if it meant being alone.

My friend's absence in the company actually created a sales opportunity because he sold equipment in addition to managing construction. I, of course, immediately saw an opportunity to take another forward step and asked if I could try my hand at selling on commission. I do not truly believe anyone thought I could make it work because I had no formal sales training, nor had I ever sold anything. On the contrary, I figured, "Hell, I sold myself into this job. I can sell anything!" When I asked if I could take a stab at the sales job, the owner laughed and said, "You know this is hard work, and you do not know anything about selling." My reply was, "Yes, but you have a lot more to gain than to lose if I *do* sell."

Well, I got the sales job, and it began a new passion that ultimately led to my future career. My willingness to work seven days a week and go way beyond the call of duty to accomplish whatever task or responsibilities were put in front of me was going to be my ticket. My mother taught me that the sooner I got a job done, the sooner I would have more time to get the next job done, and so on and so on, allowing more opportunity to make more money. If the owner of the company or the Vice President asked the sales team to go out and call on ten prospects, I went out and called on twenty. If he said we needed to increase our business by three percent, I went for six percent. I knew that if I could excel at this sales job, I could make good money. I needed to make it work. After all, I had an empty apartment, and I was alone and desperate to make my mark one way or the other. I was determined to just hang in there long enough and be persistent enough so that eventually, I would find myself in a better place.

My success was largely due to being an overachiever and having the fire in my belly to prove to myself and those around me that I could not only do the job, but I could kick everybody else's butt in the process! I grew up poor and hungry, looking at the people I worked with and feeling that they were satisfied with nothing more than a paycheck, but that was not my plan. My mother taught me early in life that a job (j-o-b) meant "Just Over Broke." Well, I had been "just over broke" my whole life with more bills than money and was ready for a change. After reading several sales books, I realized that two of the most successful ways to make money were real estate and sales. I had no money and bad credit back then, so real estate was out, but I knew I could handle selling.

So I sold and sold and sold. I actually worked seven days a week for about ten months straight. I got up about five o'clock every morning and was out the door by 5:45. I divided the state into grids and tried to find laundromats in each area. I went out and met owners, introduced myself and the company, and spread my name all over the streets so that almost every laundry owner in the entire state knew the name "Robert Renteria." I believe it took me just over a year and a half to meet and visit with almost every laundry owner, as well as several owners of dry cleaning facilities, banquet halls, nursing homes, car washes—you name it—in the state. If there were commercial washers or dryers to be found at a site, I was there, too.

I spent five years learning the business and tearing up the rubber on my car's tires by cold-calling every laundry in Illinois—that's almost 1,300 laundries, by the way. I went through many new shoes, putting more leather on the pavement than the postman, always chasing down leads and doing more door-to-door sales. Like the Pony Express in the Wild, Wild West, I rode hard all day long. I developed relationships with laundromat owners and helped them build up their businesses. I built my reputation on endless hours of hard work, many sacrifices, and a continuous commitment to my customers' dreams of business ownership and personal and financial success. I worked diligently with my customers to make sure that all the required elements for their business foundation were in place. This included understanding their short- and long-term goals and objectives. It happened so many times that a customer told me that the amount being invested was all they had, and they trusted me to help them build a successful business. I still lose sleep countless nights, just trying to cover all the bases and make sure that I am doing everything necessary to achieve the best possible results for my clients. I embrace my customers like family. I protect them from over-spending and bad leases, and from becoming over-leveraged and under-collateralized. I educate them on training their employees, marketing in their specific location and developing a competitive analysis of the surrounding marketplace, and I show them how to do everything possible to be the very best they can be as operators! This is where paying attention early on to my mentors really paid off.

I was selling commercial washers and dryers, but, really, my focus was on taking care of people—a responsibility that came naturally because of my Latino heritage and how I was raised by my mother.

Well, after really learning the "ins and outs" of the business and truly making a respectable local name for myself in the marketplace, I was promoted to a managerial position and put in charge of selling a new product line for the company. I learned that if you are going to move up, you have to be the direct cause of positively affecting the company's financial bottom line. When I had the "Top Sales Producer" title under my belt, I felt there was no stopping me.

With about six sales people, we were supposed to work at the office on Saturday rotations, but nobody wanted to work on the weekends. Nobody but me, that is! I saw weekends as another opportunity to make more money and capture more sales, cementing my number one position in the company. I actually charged the other sales reps fifty to one hundred dollars cash to pull their Saturday duty and always made more commissions than on any other day because laundromat owners who had "nine-to-five" jobs came into the company on weekends to purchase parts and to look at machines. That was my best-kept secret back then!

Finally, it seemed I had found an outlet where my personal effort, desire and passion could light up the scoreboard. About three years into the game, I found my groove. I was consistent and reached gross sales in excess of a million dollars. Sales in years four and five were somewhere between one and a half and two million dollars. My name was now known on the streets of the laundry business in Illinois. When the company had their annual sales show, probably over seventy-five percent of the owners who came to buy were there to see me. I had developed a very large core group of laundry owners who liked and wanted to deal with me. Because of the time I had spent with them discussing ways to build their businesses and solve their problems, I was the person they trusted and wanted to buy from. Initially, I'm sure plenty of owners only gave me a break because I was in my early thirties and asked them for a chance to earn their business. I had used the word "please" a lot, as in, "Please give me a chance," and most times they did. The company continued to keep me behind the scenes, never allowing me to work outside the customer pool.

Even today, the sales numbers I mentioned are a "wet dream come true" for any company who sells commercial laundry equipment. There are some companies, as a whole, that never even reach a million dollars in commercial sales. I excelled and became an important part of the company, or so I thought. Having won "Salesman of the Month" consistently and more than doubling my income from when I started, I felt I had earned the opportunity to voice my thoughts about ways to better the company's growth potential.

During this period, the executives from the various manufacturing plants came and visited our company's owner but never even gave me a passing hello, let alone two seconds of their time (what was up with that?). This bothered me because, after all, I was the number one sales rep in the company. It was well into my fourth year when I realized that I was the company's best-kept secret and that nobody outside of the company (except the laundry customers) knew who I was.

This began to chap my ass because I was working seven days a week to prove myself, but nobody from an executive level showed me any respect or appreciation at all. I started feeling bitter because there was never any acknowledgement from the so-called "bigwigs" that came in for their power meetings and first-class dinners with ownership.

Don't get me wrong—I truly appreciated the job and was grateful for my advancements within the company, but I wanted to spread my wings. I felt that I could contribute so much more if given the opportunity.

After my fourth year with the company, I approached the owner one day and asked him if I could participate in some of the future meetings with the executive staff from manufacturing. An odd look came over his face and he asked, "For what?" I explained how my daily dealings in the field with customers provided valuable information that could help us focus our sales efforts, better service our current customer base and develop more sales, thus affecting the company's bottom line. Great idea, right?

The owner looked me squarely in the eye and said with a frown, "We each have our role to play, and yours is not making executive or power decisions." He went on to say that I lacked the skills and education and that I should be happy with the job and title he had given me.

I simply said, "Okay, thank you," and humbly walked away with a sad and heavy heart. Damn, how incredibly frustrating for me, because in his eyes, the job and title were like a bone given to a dog. But I knew I had earned that position and had made many personal sacrifices to accomplish what I had during those first five years. In the end, he treated me as though he had done me a favor. To him, I was the same young man who had walked through his door five years earlier, begging him for a job. Nothing had changed.

How could he tell me that I was not worthy of making positive contributions other than just sales? I felt he was being greedy and afraid of losing his golden goose. Did he actually want me to be a prisoner of conventional wisdom? After all, I was trying to help the company. I wanted to grow and train other salesmen, sharing my successes and helping the company prosper. I wanted to be a team player, possibly even be the Vice President someday; I wanted to show the owner that I could help others drive their numbers and make sound decisions, creating a win-win for everybody. (Because that's what leaders do!)

People who succeed are not necessarily smarter; they are people who see niches and windows of opportunity. I truly felt that being on the street every day listening to customers was like having my finger on the pulse of the marketplace. Yet when I asked about making some senior managerial contributions and recommendations, he refused to discuss it—didn't even want to hear what I had to say. He had me where he wanted me and wasn't about to mess up what he thought was a good thing for his company.

Sadly enough, the day of my promotion would never come, at least not at that company. I had my own dreams of becoming an executive someday, wearing sharp suits to work, sporting a nice Rolex and driving a Mercedes Benz, getting out of my rathole apartment and buying my first home, and also being able to dine at fine restaurants. Why not? Isn't that all part of the American dream?

Like a lot of hardworking men and women, my intentions were to do a good job for the company, being loyal and honest. I learned a lot during those five years, both good and bad business practices, and I had given the job, the man and the company, my heart and soul. In the end, however, my dreams were clearly not their dreams, so I took my bag of tricks and my core group of customers and I left to paint the picture I had plastered in my mind of what I wanted to do and who I wanted to be. (I was not going to waste my time or my life!)

Like my mother always told me, "No matter what happens, the show must go on." Well, my plan was to "go on."

CHAPTER SIX

Corporate America: Keeping Up With the Big Boys

I should have figured out much earlier why the owner of the company deliberately kept me away from meetings and the folks from corporate manufacturing, and subjected me to so many racial jokes and innuendoes during those five years.

One time, we were waiting together at a restaurant for a customer, and the busboy cleaning the tables happened to be Mexican. My boss tapped me on the shoulder and said, "Hey, if things don't work out with us, maybe they will hire you." Another time, we were in the warehouse, and he asked me for my switchblade to open a box. One year, at the annual company Christmas party, he casually came over to me and whispered a snide comment in my ear, "I don't believe they will be serving tacos tonight." So many people think it's okay, that it's just "friendly joking" to make comments like this—I don't understand it.

For five years, I ignored his horrible racial comments and crude innuendos because he was paying me, but I was deeply hurt and saddened that this man would have such a shitty opinion of my people and me. The fact is that Latinos do the really crappy work in cheap labor positions because we are honest and hardworking people. Have you ever noticed that you rarely ever see a Latino begging for money with a cup on the street corners? A Mexican with no humility would rather sell bags of oranges than beg for money.

I decided to fly back to California and apply for a position with a bigger company because I had heard through the grapevine that they were looking for someone in operations and also a hotshot salesman. I got the interview and met with a man named Ben, who was the Vice President of Operations. After about half an hour, he said he felt that I would be perfect for the sales position. I then met with the sales manager, who spent ten minutes or so reviewing my resume and seemed to disregard our discussions about my track record. I then went to the office of the President of the corporation—all within one hour.

This guy was a stone-cold, arrogant, corporate asshole, and the interview did not go well at all. He said that I didn't meet the company's criteria or have the necessary credentials on my resume, so I was not a good fit. I didn't question him because he reminded me of the owner of the company that I was currently working for, and I could not stomach putting myself back into that situation. I sure as hell was not looking to replace old pain with new pain! The meeting lasted less than five minutes, after which I gracefully thanked him for his time and excused myself. As I walked down the hallway in stunned silence, Ben stopped me and asked what had happened. I told him how the interview went, and he was simply appalled! He asked me for my cell phone number and reiterated the fact that he really felt good about me and thought I had exactly what they needed and were looking for. We shook hands, and he wished me well. Ben then put his hand on my shoulder and said, "I **won't** forget you."

At this juncture, I couldn't help but wonder if this was what the laundry industry and the business world was really all about—being judged simply on the basis of your "paper" credentials and surname. I was bewildered. What about hard work, loyalty, honesty, and a proven track record? I got on a plane with pure disgust and headed back to Chicago.

About three months later, I received an unexpected call from Ben. He told me that the guy who refused to hire me because I did not have the "right stuff" had been fired. (How is that for not having the right stuff?) Ben went on to say that a friend and professional colleague named Hal had become President of a very large, privately held organization on the East Coast that had plans of perhaps becoming a publicly traded company in the future. He wanted to know if I was still actively looking for something new. Shortly thereafter, Hal called and told me he was flying into Chicago in about two weeks, and he wondered if I would meet with him to discuss a sales and management position with his company.

I was at O'Hare Airport bright and early that morning at seven o'clock, spit and polished, wearing a sweet black double-breasted suit, looking like a million bucks when he arrived. We shook hands and went to sit in the Admiral's room. Hal just sat there for a few minutes and did not say a word. I asked if there was anything he wanted to know about me or anything he wanted to talk about specifically as it related to the sales position.

Hal said, "No, Robert. I just wanted to come to Chicago, look in your eyes and see if you are still that same hungry guy with a burning fire in your belly that met Ben about three and a half months back."

"Well, what do you see?" I asked.

Looking me squarely in the eye, he smiled and said, "How would you like to come work for us?" Hal went on to tell me that Ben had given me a five-star rating. He said he wanted a sales professional who was strong, confident and hungry, not some so-called "marquee sales pro" who thought the world owed him a nice cushion simply because Mommy and Daddy had paid for him to attend an Ivy League college. It was my guess that he and Ben went back several years, and that Hal respected Ben's ability to size up talent. "I know this is going to work," he kept repeating. "You're the real deal, Robert." He said that he had already done his homework and was anxious for me to start.

I asked him what exactly I would be doing.

He laughed and said, "Well, first you will be selling here in Illinois, and then I want the rest of the company to get a taste of you."

When I asked what he meant by that, Hal explained that given my track record, he believed I would be contagious, and he eventually thought I would run the commercial sales division of the company. He wanted me to create a team of ferocious, hard-charging "Roberts." We discussed a generous compensation plan, and I agreed to his offer on all counts. After meeting with the entire executive staff and giving them "a taste of Robert," the job was mine! There was never any discussion nor any questions about my paper credentials or what college I had attended. Their sole interest was whether I could build a strong sales force. I told them that there are five guarantees in life. The first two are death and taxes. Third and fourth were that "there is a God, and I'm not him." Number five, I explained, was that I would not just build a sales team, but a band of brothers.

When I returned from the East Coast, I gave a two-week notice to my employer and explained that I had an opportunity to climb the corporate ladder with greater financial opportunities and a broader range of managerial responsibilities. My boss assured me that I would never make it there and then pleaded, "We are a family" (as if that made any sense). He insisted that I was making a mistake and wondered who I was kidding. He even went so far as to tell me that I "owed him," and I should feel obligated to stay.

"I don't owe you anything," I said. "And you don't own me. Nobody owns me." In that moment, I knew my only mistake up to that point was not leaving sooner.

So now, I was starting yet another phase in life: cashing in on a relentless effort to throw my hat into the corporate arena. How is that for a poor ex-homeboy from East Los Angeles! My heritage would serve me well during those days, simply working hard and being honest. I needed to prove that I had what it took to not only play with the best and beat the best, but to become *the* best in the entire industry. Corporate America, ready or not, here I come!

Education is the best way for Hispanics to level the playing field, but in my case, I would have to use my street smarts to pull off this opportunity. I knew good and well that by undertaking this venture, I was going to be way out of my element and in over my head because I did not have the business background, training or paper pedigree. What I realized, though, was that as long as I used my street smarts, sales abilities and industry contacts to impact the company's bottom line, I would stand out above my colleagues. Basically, it was going to be baptism by fire.

In January 1996, I started my new position and immediately began to light up the scoreboard by delivering huge sales numbers. At the close of the first quarter, the executive staff immediately flew to Chicago to discuss future acquisitions with me and talk about me leading the charge for their commercial sales division. (Hal was right!)

As they say, "Let the games begin." I was promoted after only a few months to a managerial position, and the game was on. Soon after, I took over one region after another, increasing the territories state-by-state with my team, growing the sales representatives. The sales numbers immediately followed at a rapid pace.

When starting this new position in 1996, I was working solely in Illinois. Shortly after becoming a manager, however, I took over a Missouri company that the corporation had purchased; the new territory also covered Memphis and part of Arkansas. Shortly thereafter, the company went public, and I was on the move—living the corporate jet-set lifestyle, flying from city to city and covering all of Florida, New York, Atlanta, Alabama, Massachusetts, Wisconsin, Indiana, South Carolina, Connecticut, Rhode Island and international sales within the Bahamas and several other islands in the Caribbean.

Although the sales numbers were growing at a staggering pace, I managed to develop a solid team of sales professionals that bonded closely together, which was an absolute advantage considering how far I was geographically from everyone. This made it easier for me to rely on their integrity and execute my sales plan effectively. These men really did come together like a true band of brothers.

We had a very cohesive relationship, much like what I had experienced in the military. They thought they worked for me but in reality, I worked for them, making sure they had the ammunition (sales leads) and firepower (support) they needed to go to battle and compete on a daily basis. I put myself and my job on the line—unafraid, risking everything, and gambling on the strength and character of these men and their willingness to follow my leadership. They didn't just shine solely for the company's benefit, but for the pride and integrity of the team as a whole. In leading them, I promised that we would grow together as I executed my plan, and I can say wholeheartedly that everyone in the "Renteria army" succeeded. They bought into the sales philosophy of Robert Renteria, the same philosophy that I had tried sharing with my former employer. It was a pretty exciting time for everyone! You have to take your chance when it comes, and I took that chance on several men who didn't have impressive paper credentials, but who displayed, in some form or another, a mirror image of myself—a very hungry guy with raw talent and fire in his belly. This group of aggressive, but so-called undereducated men, proved to be, by far, the best commercial laundry sales force in the entire country during that period.

I was well into a six-figure income with lots of perks, and most of my men were doubling their salaries as well—a few of them had even tripled their incomes.

The company was acquiring other companies on a continuous basis throughout my tenure as Vice President of Commercial Sales, and it was my responsibility to develop these areas by hiring good people and kicking the numbers in the ass.

At the end of the first year, I was personally the company's top-producing sales professional with the most sales and highest profit margins. I won every award offered at the annual sales meeting that year. Sales representatives from every region across the country were there to witness this East Los Angeles homeboy showing those Ivy League "blue suits" how it's done, Latino style! I was on fire, kicking ass and taking names. This is where I showed those Gumbies how to separate the men from the boys. I felt like a cat burglar—I had stolen the show, and it was definitely one of the best years of my life.

I led the charge in what panned out to be a record-breaking year in sales for the company and did so without any guidance or supervision. It was literally a one-man show, and guess who was calling the shots. Me. As the company successfully went through the Initial Public Offering (IPO), I stayed focused on driving the numbers and participated in the acquisition of several companies. During those six years of loyal and dedicated service, I set up my part of the company, developing new commercial sales business both nationally and internationally and by far, again, the best commercial laundry sales team across the United States. It's important to remember that the difference between winning and losing is preparation.

I was now all over the national trade publications. I became a face within the industry and a voice to be reckoned with. I was elected unanimously to the Coin Laundry Chicago Board of Directors and sat in boardroom meetings making decisions that would impact the direction of our industry.

There I was, just 36 years old, swinging it with the so-called "big boys." I felt good knowing I had not listened to the so-called "professionals" and industry cronies who had told me time and time again that I did not have the credentials or qualifications to be in the number one spot. I didn't take "no" for an answer from anyone, and instead drew a deep line in the sand and made the decision that this was my time. As long as I had the opportunity to climb into the ring, I was going to take the gloves off and knock out anyone who tried giving me any shit or getting in my way.

The only thing better than a good salesman, I learned, was a good salesman who was pissed off, so I seized the chance to lead and help people realize what they could become. I made it a point to hire blue-collar people who would otherwise not have the opportunity because they lacked paper pedigrees or credentials. My team consisted of many guys who were poor, but they were smart, hungry and very hardworking, and they realized that this was their opportunity to trade in their blue collars for white collars. This "secret recipe"—the men I called my "Band of Brothers"—worked their asses off for me. We were our own little Renteria army and we took the industry by storm, like a bunch of stealth bombers. I'd been told that only angels know how to fly, but you should have seen us soar! Riding with my sales force was pure magic.

During my reign as Vice President of the company, I never asked, "Is this okay?" or "Is that okay?" I just did what needed to be done because I figured it was a lot easier to beg for forgiveness than to ask for permission. When it comes to big business, money is very forgiving.

During my second year, I received a sizable bonus for my sales commissions. Some of the other managers and executives in the company asked me, "Robert, what are you going to do with all that money?" Not that it was any of their business, but I told them I was going to fly home and fulfill a promise I had made as a child to my mother. I flew home over the 1997 Christmas holidays, invited her to lunch and told her that I wanted to talk with her. I had wrapped up a small gift bag that I gave to her over lunch. "Merry Christmas," I told her.

She asked me what it was, and I told her to guess. She suspected it might be jewelry because she had wanted a necklace, so she looked confused when she finally unwrapped her gift bag and saw the set of keys to a brand new car. *"Mijo,"* she said. "What is this?"

I looked at my mother with a big smile and a lump in my throat and said, "Mamá, this means you will never have to take a bus again!" She busted out crying and yes, I broke down as well. That was a big day for the both of us. I don't believe I could ever truly capture in words the pride I felt at that exact moment; being able to keep a promise I had made some thirty-two years prior as a five-year-old little boy to his mother. (Remember, your word is your bond, your word is who you are.)

I traveled a lot, and it was exactly what I had always wanted for myself. I was working in corporate America and was now a Vice President of the company and one of the most popular guys in the industry. I started writing articles for the trade publications, and I was soon recognized as the expert in the business. Many suppliers and manufacturers started calling me the "WashPro," and I became recognized both nationally and internationally as a world-class coin laundry professional.

In 1999, I was asked to speak on a distribution panel at a national convention in Las Vegas, Nevada, to share my broad industry knowledge with hundreds of investors looking to join the industry globally. I also participated in Florida in 1997 and in New Orleans in 2001, where I had the opportunity to speak directly to several investors and distributors who sought my expert advice.

In 2001, I was probably one of, if not *the* highest paid guy in the entire industry. It just so happened that I was also an eight hundred-pound gorilla living the dream of many men and women who aspire to climb the broken ladder of corporate America. I had what all of them wanted: a hefty salary with bonuses and an impressive title attached to it, a sizable expense account and a car allowance for a luxury vehicle. Wow! What's not to like?

The experience, although a wonderful learning curve in life, became jaded for me as time went on. I allowed myself to become a statistic, a mere number. The human element was far removed, and I was not being true to myself. I nearly forgot who I was down deep inside. I knew that it was time to get back to what I loved—people.

Latinos are extremely loyal and honest individuals who take care of each other; at least that's how it was in my family. In business, you have to be tough, but the politics and posturing, and the fact that only the numbers mattered, began to get the better of me. I began to see casualties. A lot of people suffered unnecessarily, meaning customers who were being oversold and businesses that were bleeding and failing for the wrong reasons. I reached a point where I couldn't live with myself anymore because we were making (taking) money off people as if we were some kind of goddamned vultures. I'd learned in the military that we "leave no man behind," but they don't often play by this golden rule in most big businesses. My sales representatives, myself and, most importantly, our customers (the ones who were actually writing our paychecks) had all become expendable. It was all about black and white, all about the numbers, but for me it was about right and wrong. Even within this dark, unspoken side of corporate America, I became an executive with a moral conscience.

Since I was a young boy, I always dreamed of living a better life and getting out of the ghetto (the barrio of East Los Angeles). I wanted to be respected and admired, and to influence people's lives in a positive way. Without a doubt, I had come to a crossroads in my corporate life. For six years, I gave my all for the company and had no personal life. I was over two thousand miles away from my family and loved ones. I was disconnected from reality, trying only to impress the executive staff and show everyone that I was the man. For what?

I was in and out of airports, sleeping in different cities every week—which was great in the beginning, but I started thinking about some of the men and women I knew who had retired. We took them to a farewell dinner and maybe bought them a watch for their many years of loyal service. I felt that it degraded people who had dedicated their lives to a corporation, only to have it suddenly end like that.

I was clearly disenchanted. So now, with no need to be validated, the only person to whom I had something to prove was myself. It's no wonder I had a free run at what I was doing for the company. I worked seven days a week, averaging twelve to sixteen hours a day, driving the numbers year after year, exceeding targets and goals simply for smiles and pats on the back. I knew I would never really fit in and become one of the "good old boys." Every farmer needs a mule, and I realized that was what I was. They were going to let me plow the field as long as I had the desire to run the numbers, the numbers and more numbers.

I remember waking up one morning and not knowing where in the hell I was. I had become exhausted to the point that I thought I was having a heart attack. (It turned out to be an anxiety attack.) Again, for what? The company was well aware that I was working myself into an early grave. I let them know that I was on the verge of a mental meltdown and asked for help on several occasions, but there was never any offer of assistance. The hypocritical, horseshit stock answer was always, "It's not in the budget." Yeah, right!

My sales team was the real reason I hung around, because they and their families were very important to me and had become a huge part of my life. Looking forward from that point, I felt that the only way to be true to myself was to take the next step in life and open my own company. Why not? Why be a mule? If I was going to work my ass off, I could do it for myself and the people we were supposed to be helping—our customers!

I remember calling home and having a conversation with my mother. She was shocked. "Oh, *mijo!*" she exclaimed. "Are you sure? You have worked so hard to get where you are."

I told her that I didn't want to be some old man sitting in a bar one day saying, "I wish I would have..." or "I wonder if I could have..." I grew up around many family members and listened to strangers and friends who frequently sat in bars, drinking and telling stories, and they never made it from the barrio to the board room. Now I could look back and say, "I did that!" I could proudly proclaim that I had played with the so-called "best" and beat them at their own game, by their rules.

I was taught that if you are ever going to make a move, it's best to do so while you're on top so that you are more marketable. *Why not?* I thought. Many people told me that I was the best, most "connected" guy in the industry, and it had worked for me in the past.

In the spring of 2001, I made the million-dollar phone call and told the executive management that I was going to hold myself to a higher standard. I told them that I felt my time there was done, and I was going to be moving on. Although my six years there, in my opinion, was time well-wasted, I wish our parting had been friendlier but let's just say it was very much like getting divorced. (For me, it was a bitter but sweet ending.)

My life up to that point had been one big race toward what I thought I wanted, chasing dead presidents and scaling to the top of the corporate ladder. In the end, I discovered that corporate America was filled with a lot of educated derelicts engaged in a "survival of the un-fittest" game. I learned that the faces changed, but the game remained the same, and simply having a degree did not make a person better qualified. Although education is very important and can be a great equalizer for any race, it's my opinion that performance, hands down, is the biggest asset.

For the next six years after making it to the corporate world in 1996, it became obvious to me that many employees frequently drank to relieve the stress and anxiety of the daily pressures that come with managerial or high profile positions. It's not easy making quotas, keeping a department under budget, wasting hours in strategy meetings and then firing people because it's always someone else's fault when things aren't going right. (Hmm.) Coupled with the stress, it seemed that any reason to entertain customers or prospects was merely an excuse to get to the barroom and indulge in alcohol, all the while calling it a business expense. That was, at least, my view on how several companies did things. Many times, we stayed out until two in the morning, and then came into the boardroom at eight o'clock to make a presentation while still half "in the bag," with bloodshot eyes and a fog of drunken whiskey breath. Life became nothing less than battling the demons with alcohol.

Based on my life experiences, coming from a man who spent many hours with friends and family in barrooms, people in the business and corporate world are no different than we were in the barrio except for the job, money, education and fine clothing.

I don't regret my experience in corporate America, and I am glad I had the opportunity to show the business world that a person can be a shining star and succeed at any level regardless of race, age, education or professional training if only given the opportunity. The milestones I achieved in my industry had never been accomplished before, nor duplicated since. This proves that if you don't give up and maintain hope and believe in yourself, anybody can make it happen!

My "boardroom" experiences were many and unique, and I am proud of myself for holding onto my morals and my integrity. It was never about the money for me, not just back then, but even today, and I never measured people's success by what they had or by the size of their pocketbook. Success is not having what you want, but wanting what you've got.

For me, it came down to being unwilling to sell out and make a deal with the devil just to be a star in hell! I wanted to do it right or not do it at all. In good conscience, I walked away with my dignity, a strong sense of decency and my head held high, with pride and my soul intact. At one time, I believed that being a business executive in the corporate world would give me respect. Instead, I learned that the only respect I needed in this lifetime was self-respect, and I took mine with me. (Follow your heart.)

So I cut bait with the company I had helped build for six years and took a giant leap of faith in my own abilities. I stepped away from the hard-partying sales trips, all the wild women and alcohol-filled nights that were so much like my childhood in the barrio of L.A.—and I opened my own business.

My success had come from performance, planning, faith and bottom-line hard work. I was ready to turn the page and focus on making my dream of business ownership a reality.

WASH PRO TAKES THE SHOT

Industry-acclaimed coin laundry professional, Robert J. Renteria Jr., goes swimming with the sharks!

Making the
——————— American Dream ———————
a Reality

Robert Renteria built Angel's first laundromat in 1992 and a second in 1995. Ten years later, in 2005 Robert built him a third laundry. This laundry is approximately 6000 square feet, and one of the five largest laundries in the state of Illinois. This laundry is also one of the highest volume producing laundries in the USA.

Long time customer and friend Angel Reynoso with Robert

CHAPTER SEVEN

The Dream: Being My Own Boss

Toward the end of 2001, I officially decided to go into business for myself. I took the past eleven years of hard work and endless efforts and threw my hat into the arena to compete with the seven other well-established laundry companies in Illinois. I had already clearly proven myself both nationally and internationally, so this progression seemed like a natural next step.

When the rumors got out that I was going to open a distribution company, there was a lot of skepticism from the other companies.

Although rumors circulated that my new partner and I had this elaborate master plan, our partnership was truly a coincidence. Even so, the dynamics, talent and synergy were, in our opinion, an explosion waiting to happen! During our discussions, we decided that if we were going to do this, we were going to do it right. We shared many of the same ideas, values, business practices and principles at the time, and sure enough, we had a deal.

Our first task after agreeing to partner up, while sitting at my kitchen table, was to name the company. After seeing my Mercedes convertible parked in the driveway with a license plate that read "WashPro," he looked at me with a grin. Of course, we named the company WashPro.

The narcissism and criticisms thrown around by our competitors were based on fear and uncertainty. Rumors said that we would not last a year, that we were "trunk slammers" selling a no-name product, etc.

We launched our company in December 2001, agreeing to be customer-focused and provide a brand of personalized care with tailored business services and products to enhance the productivity and profitability of our laundry customers. We took the lessons we learned over the years and avoided the pitfalls that we had collectively witnessed in our industry.

A customer I've personally worked with now for almost twenty-one years asked me what I was planning to do when I left corporate America. I shared with him my plans to open my own business. He said to come and see him when that happened, so when I finally got to that point, I called him and we set an appointment. I arrived for our scheduled meeting on a Sunday night about eleven o'clock, after he closed his grocery store, and we went downstairs to his basement office so that we could talk privately. We sat down and he congratulated me on taking a big step—being bold enough to jump into an existing pool of sharks that already had very established businesses. He thanked me for standing by him over the years and explained to me that no one else in our industry had shown him the respect he felt he deserved because he was from Mexico and did not speak very good English. He told me he truly trusted me and felt that I was the only one who had given him the time and respect he deserved. He then reached over, opened a floor safe, and placed a very large sum of money on the table. He said he wanted to be our first customer and that he and his family wanted to bless our business. I was overwhelmed, choked up without any words other than, "Thank you." We stood up and put our arms around one another. Needless to say, we have become the best of friends, and family as well. I held my composure and fell just short of tears at that moment. He said that he was proud of me and that he had enjoyed watching my career go from being a sales representative to an executive in corporate America to now owning my own distribution company. He said that I not only made *him* proud, but every Latino, as well as anyone else who dares to dream! This man was exactly one of the many kinds of business owners who believed in me and supported me throughout my career. My philosophy about business over the years was based on mutually shared success and personal relationships, not just selling merchandise. I truly love and respect my customers as family.

Perhaps largely due to my own vanity, I grossly underestimated the hours required to get our company off the ground. I've also licked a lot more envelopes than I care to admit. I recall burning the midnight oil, sometimes e-mailing and faxing back and forth with customers until well past one in the morning, drinking several cups of coffee and trying to stay awake as we filled in the voids and worked together to generate sales. It is very important, for those of you who are thinking about starting your own business, that you do your due diligence and have your full family support behind you. (There is strength in numbers.)

Initially, we undertook a huge direct mail campaign to let everyone in the industry know that we had launched WashPro and that existing laundromat owners would deal directly with me.

The strategy was to market ourselves rather than the equipment because, after all, people really do buy from people. We used our already high-profile names, and the marketing effort was a smashing success, which surprised everyone but us.

At one time or another over the years, I had serviced nearly all of the customers. Because we had done it so well, the response was truly remarkable. We immediately began selling washers, dryers and ancillary products, and we developed new laundromats and brokered existing laundries. It was a very well-rounded platform.

Now, perhaps that makes it sound a lot easier than it really was, but our competitors were blindsided and in total disbelief. I constantly heard that our customers were being asked, "Why are you buying from these guys? They have no-name products. We have the best products, and we are the bigger company!" The industry, however, had fallen prey to what we had gambled on—

they were simply selling iron, but we were selling ourselves and our extensive knowledge. Customers wanted to work with us. We have impeccable reputations, and we treat our customers like gold. While we were out dining at fine steak and seafood restaurants, the competitors were trying to entertain the same customers at small coffee and doughnut shops. (Hmm.) It did not take long for the customers to realize who would treat them with the standards and respect they deserved. More importantly, we had already made money in this business and could teach them how to do the same. While the entire industry was telling customers and investors that they had the best washers, we were holding investment seminars educating anyone who would listen and leaving them with the confidence that we had the credentials and experience to assist them in making their dreams of successful business ownership come true. Knowledge is power! (Looking back now, I believe it was destiny that brought the two of us together.)

Our industry is manufacturer-driven, meaning it's all about moving iron and feeding the monster. That's exactly the reason I left corporate America, because the human element was far removed and everybody became "just a number." I have a nasty taste for this type of selling, which is why I continue to say that economics and ethics are a bad mix.

We had a very busy first year trying to make our place as a new company in Illinois and Indiana. We successfully survived wading through all the insanity that goes with starting up any new business.

We had hired our first sales employee during that year, and after working out of our home offices and streamlining everything we could by outsourcing, we opened our official headquarters in April 2003. WashPro now had an exceptional home with a smooth and polished contemporary atmosphere that was designed for educational seminars and business-to-business coaching. Most conventional distributors were set up more like car dealerships, with washers and dryers on display throughout the business area. We had a state-of-the-art business center that reeked of money. When people walked into the WashPro business center, they smiled because they smelled opportunity! WashPro was now deemed a success, and it wasn't long before the critics were silenced for good.

Now with a thirty-five hundred square-foot business center in place, we began selectively recruiting sales representatives that would mold well into our model of business-to-business strategic partnerships. By the end of 2004, we had nine "sales pros" working under the arm of WashPro. This made our company the largest sales force in commercial coin laundry distribution in the Midwest. By the end of the same year, we had also developed the largest brokerage division for coin laundries. We had diversified the company in 2003 by going against the grain in conventional distribution, as it was known, and by creating a true "one-stop shop" for anyone getting into the business, already in the business, or simply getting out of the business.

In 2004, after only three years, we were awarded the most productive and highest volume-producing distributor in the United States. Robert Renteria, who was once an eight hundred-pound gorilla, had again raised his game to another new level—an exalted status of success. The man once told to "mind his place" in the world was elected President and Chairman for IPSO USA in 2004, 2005 and again in 2006, representing distributors on a national level. (How's that for not having so-called credentials!) My education came from the streets of hard-knocks, giving me a master's degree in kicking ass and taking names.

At the end of 2005, WashPro was chosen by *American Coin-Op Magazine* to have built and designed the most beautiful coin laundry in the entire United States, and the award was published in the January 2006 edition.

Lightning had definitely struck twice, and Robert Renteria was back on top as one of the faces of the coin laundry industry, receiving a plethora of awards and accolades. Again, I became a poster boy for a national marketing campaign by the manufacturer; selling dreams rather than products seemed to have caught fire. The phenomenon caught many of the other manufacturers asleep at the wheel—naively and foolishly still believing that people really give a shit about washers and dryers.

I was again being interviewed and recognized as the "industry acclaimed coin laundry professional" and began authoring articles that were being published in trade publications on a regular basis.

There was no one now, corporate or otherwise, who could deny me or try taking any credit for my personal achievements and accomplishments. This was mine and mine alone, and it gave me great pleasure knowing that no one could ever take it away from me. I was not going to allow anyone to keep me as his or her "best-kept secret" anymore. Since opening my own business, it has sometimes been difficult competing against much larger companies with many more years behind them, but we have remained true to our business model and true to our customers, which is just one reason why we continue to grow.

I was asked recently what I could point to that best explains why we have successfully overcome the obvious obstacles mentioned. I took a line out of an old Rocky movie. "In order to beat me, he's going to have to kill me. But to do that, he's got to stand in front of me and be willing to die himself, and I don't know if he's going to be willing to do that."

This fierce attitude on our part separates the men from the boys and gives us the edge as we go out with a vengeance to build dreams, keep our company moving forward and make the cash register ring everyday.

I am very blessed and grateful that several customers have remained with me throughout the years. They are huge supporters and continue to believe in me. I have been very loyal in return by always staying in touch and regularly checking to make sure that they are okay and continuing to build their businesses.

I have given my life to pursuing and living the American dream, and I am proud to say that it has never been solely about the money. I believed that if I were willing to work hard and smart, the money would eventually be there. Too many people are in the game for the wrong reasons, meaning they are simply trying to make a fast buck. There are no shortcuts. You can't just pour some powder into a glass, stir it up and have it instantly become a pocket full of dough. My mother told me that the secret to success was hard work, and I never forgot or lost sight of that. I didn't just wake up great. I devoted the time, I earned my stripes, and I put in the hard work necessary to get there.

The basis of my own success has always remained the same: if I took care of the people who were my customers, I would see the fruits for my efforts. When my customers are safe and their businesses are on a solid financial foundation, only then do I get paid. You must be loyal and true to the people who help you along the way, as well as being true to yourself.

There is no "I" in team, which means that it isn't about ME (or you, if you have employees). It is about training and empowering employees to be accountable; it's about allowing them to stand tall and prove themselves as individuals. This is very important, especially if you plan to grow your business.

Building a team is critical and it's a "do or die" if your company is going to survive in today's aggressive, competitive, dog-eat-dog world. Being resourceful and having good people skills is also imperative, especially if you want customer retention and repeat business. This means you must *genuinely* and *passionately* listen to your customers' goals and objectives, map out a plan, and then roll up your sleeves and get down and dirty to help each other across the finish line.

There must also be nothing less than a one hundred and fifty percent commitment (nothing half-assed) if you are going to leave your current job and be bold and ambitious enough to start up your own business. You must be willing to make many, many sacrifices if you want to separate yourself from the conventional wisdom of today's business world. You will work very late hours, sometimes all night long, including weekends and holidays; you will definitely miss family events, parties, etc. But you must do it if you hope to someday feel the same pride and satisfaction that I do every time I walk into our business center and see the Wash-Pro name on the front door and on our wall in the lobby. *That* feeling is sometimes beyond words. I admit that the hours, the sleepless nights and the ongoing concerns for our customers are sometimes overwhelming, but it's all worth it, especially when a customer puts their arms around me, looks me in the eye and says, "Thank you for making our dreams of owning our own business come true!"

I know exactly how my customers feel, because *they* helped *me* make my business ownership dream come true, and they helped make my dream of being one of the only Latino business owners in this industry come true, too!

The benefits and financial rewards in owning a business allow you the opportunity to ultimately provide a better standard of living than the one where you began. My fire in the belly is driven by my mother, who always encouraged me to do my best and to be smart enough to turn my pain, cuts and bruises into my battle cries.

I learned to never let anyone tell me that I can't do something. If that had been the case in my own personal journey, I would have probably ended up like my real father—dead on skid row. Instead, I used all of my negative life experiences as a fuel to drive me. The anger I had buried deep inside was the rage that propelled me to go forward, and it helped me get beyond the scars and skeletons that haunted me throughout my lifetime. I wanted to show all of those people, both in my personal life and in my career, that I was not going to take a back seat to someone else because I lacked a formal "book" education or because of my Spanish surname. Nor was I going to settle for going to a Super Bowl for second place—that Super Bowl would be a game for losers, and I am not a loser. I am a winner, and I am never going to be satisfied with anything less than winning! (There is a champion that lies within YOU.)

The Latino culture, which has been viewed as a minority, is now a majority. Whether this world is ready or not, look out, baby, because, not only here we come, but we're already here! Looking back over the past twenty-one years of my business journey, I can say that there were times when I thought that maybe, just maybe, it all seemed too difficult and I should find something else to do. But sitting here today, I can tell you that no matter how hard it gets, you **can't** give in and you **can't** give up. NEVER let go of your dreams! Have the intellectual fortitude, perseverance and dedication to hang in there, even after others let go. You may even want to consider yourself and your quest as I do mine, like a junkie looking for his next (business) fix!

Every morning before I go to work, I close my eyes and I take the time to remember where I came from, and I think of all of the hard work it took to get me here. I tell myself every day that "the window of opportunity is open and this is my time!"

I am very proud of what I have accomplished so far, yet I remain humble and grounded as I continue to feed my hunger and reach for new plateaus. I remain "myself," regardless of where I've been or where I will yet be. I do not feel as though I have fully arrived. In fact, I am praying that my books "From the Barrio to the Board Room" and "Mi Barrio" will impact more than just a niche market like the one I service today, but instead touches every corner of the US and countries all around the world.

During my entire career, I have never sold out and was never willing to conform to being a "yes, sir" man. My Latino upbringing and my military experience helped me understand that you have to help people and be compassionate for others. Because I have never seen an ATM machine attached to the back of a hearse (meaning: you can't take it with you), I gave back along the way to an endless amount of people. This may have cost me financially in the short term, but I never fell prey to the "corporate greed" philosophy. My unselfishness has paid me back in bundles, not just monetarily, but also by enriching my soul. I have always believed that if you give with your hand and your heart open, you'll get it back tenfold. The funny thing is, now that I have become a name in my industry, the people who criticized me as I passed them along the way are the same back-stabbing assholes who are sucking my kneecaps, trying to get my business, pretending they are my friends and telling me, with their halfhearted smiles, that they want to help me now. These same guys wouldn't offer me a cup of coffee ten years ago, and today are all transparent "kiss-asses." I have only one final comment for all the folks who snubbed me, disrespected and antagonized me along the way (and if you're reading this book, you know who you are): how do you like me now? In business, as in life, everybody wants to be your friend when you're on top. It's when the chips are down and you are at your lowest point that you find out who your true friends really are.

I believe in redemption, and because I cared about people and represented the underdog, God has been good to me. Our most valuable commodity is time. Remember that yesterday doesn't exist. Try to make the most of every minute. Time is money.

I've had my moments and my many days in the sun. I realize that I wouldn't be here unless God had opened all of these doors to me. Oddly enough, all of the things I did over the past twenty-one years were exactly the things people kept telling me could not be done. In the end, I'd like to believe that I'll be remembered as the guy they never saw coming, and as the man who made a difference by helping others to raise the bar and elevate the game to a whole new set of standards.

AFTERWORD

You, Too, Can Chase the American Dream!

My entire life, people from the old neighborhoods I lived in (even my so-called friends) laughed at me when I tried telling them my ideas of what I wanted from my life, such as a college education, maybe a business someday, a big home on a pond or a Mercedes-Benz. So many of them were just jealous or "haters." Not enough people in life simply say, "Hey, good idea! Go for it! Good luck! Why not? Congratulations!" Instead, I always heard a lot of, "You wish! Stop dreaming! Get real! Who are you kidding! You're going to screw it up! Yeah, right! Just get a job! Shut the hell up! You ain't never gonna be shit!"

I spent my youth bombarded with negative images and influences everywhere I turned. The idea of crawling out of dire poverty was wishful thinking and, sadly enough, that mindset continues to keep people in the armpit of our barrios and ghettos today.

In my life, it would have been very easy to concede and simply accept the cards that were dealt to me, allowing the environment in which I grew up to dictate my future. Not everyone in life is either blessed or lucky enough to be born outside of poverty, so we each need to make a choice and either decide to accept such circumstances as our future or decide we're going to stand up and change the direction of our lives by doing something about it.

Once I understood that life was whatever I wanted it to be, I ignored the "haters." I figured out that if I just used my tenacity, dared to dream and had the guts to take a shot at pursuing those dreams, I could be much more than others thought of me. I would never know how good I could be unless I stood up, pulled the trigger and tried!

I made that decision and never looked back. I ignored the people in my path who tried creating reasons why I was not good enough or who thought that I was kidding myself because I had dreams, big dreams. Throughout my life, my mother made me feel that if there was something I could see in my mind, it was possible for me to achieve it. She told me that there are no victims, only those who refuse to make a choice.

From my humble beginnings as a child growing up in East L.A., throughout my years as a teenager, in the military, eventually in corporate America, and even now in my own business, there have always been and will continue to be people who hate, because that's just the way it is. It's sad but true.

If the cliché "You are what you eat" is true, then "What we think is what we become," is equally true. We need to focus on wealth rather than debt. Getting ahead in life needs to be a top priority for every man, woman and child. Although what we strive for may seem like a million miles away at times, there is absolutely no reason to accept living a mediocre lifestyle. There is so much more to life than living paycheck-to-paycheck, swimming in debt and performing back-breaking work for chump change with the mere hopes of "maybe" only gaining a high school education (you deserve everything life has to offer). I am living proof that there is a big difference between simply living and living well.

There is no longer any reason to work our fingers to the bone, barely scraping by and living hand-to-mouth, particularly when we live in a time when an abundance of opportunities exist that allow each of us to go for the gold. We can all achieve great success despite overwhelming odds, and there is nothing out of reach! If we have faith in ourselves, there's no limit to how far we can go. (You have to see yourself there!)

If you fail, which I have many times in my life, you must get up, dust the dirt off your knees and try again and again until you get to your goal, whatever it is. You need to write your goals and objectives down on paper. Then, just like taking a road trip, you have to map out the path that will get you from point "A" to point "B" and beyond.

What I'm telling you is that you can't play darts blindfolded. In other words, you can't hit a target you can't see, and you also can't reach a goal you don't have.

I confess that I've sinned and done some bad things I never dreamed I would do. I also made plenty of mistakes and suffered many disappointments on my journey, sometimes drinking shots of whiskey and drowning my sorrows in self-pity all night in some smoky barroom looking for the answers at the bottom of a bottle. I am here to tell you that the answer is not at the bottom of the bottle. Your answer is within YOU, just as I carried mine inside of me. You must trust in God and trust those in your family who love you. Most of all, you must believe in yourself and in making the most of the talents you were blessed with at birth.

Many people think that life is all about luck. I suppose that may be partly true. Certainly, with a lot of hard work and persistence, you sometimes create your own luck along the way, but in the end, the results come from a very precise, deliberate plan that you make a daily and relentless effort to execute effectively.

Taking the first step is scary, I know, especially when you think you're out there all alone. (Believe me when I tell you, you're NOT alone.) Once you get some momentum, though, and find yourself in a groove, it's actually quite a rush! So it's then, and only then, that you go from being employed to being empowered.

My life has been an ongoing process of creating the man I am today, watching and learning from many successful men and women who touched and inspired me while I tried to find my own way. I have never been jealous of other people's successes; I embraced them as educational and motivational building blocks in my own journey. Growing up, I had no positive male figures in my life showing me the way. My mother, bless her, was more of a crutch than a role model, but she always supported everything and anything I wanted to do and served as my greatest emotional anchor.

I believe the ultimate "role model" is the world itself and all of the tangible things it has to offer.

Do not allow fear to overcome your emotions and stifle your desire to move forward. Even when you are scared, you need to push ahead anyway, letting that fear drive you. Failure will never overtake you if your determination to succeed is strong enough. Taking calculated chances is what life is all about (risk vs. reward), so don't be afraid to follow your heart and trust your instincts. If you are willing to look fear in the face, you will find out just what kind of man or woman, boy or girl, you really are. I admit that I've been scared, intimidated and afraid, but I never stopped dreaming and never stopped believing in testing the limits of the human heart. As long as we have a *corazon* (heart), we always have a chance. (We always have a chance!)

The world is a tough and crazy place. You'll have regrets about some of the choices you make in life, but you have to believe. Belief is like air—you can't see it, but you need it to survive! No matter where you come from and no matter who you are, no matter your age, the length of your hair, color of your skin or gender, if you are willing to do whatever it takes (legally) and you want it badly enough, you will be able to overcome seemingly impossible obstacles. (Believe me I know.)

You have to believe in yourself and decide if you're going to be a Rottweiler or a rat, a man or a mouse, a shark or a guppy.

Remember that if you believe, there is **always** a way!

You need to have courage, go after your dreams and never take no for an answer. No guts, no glory, as they say. Don't ever let anyone tell you that you cannot do something. If that had been the case for me, I'd likely still be a product of my past environment and still be living in the barrio. (You have to think for yourself.)

Your word is your bond; your word is who you are. Like building a house, you must build your reputation on a solid foundation. In building your castle (your life), you must build a foundation based on principles of stone rather than sand and be willing to live with the price you pay for the life you choose. From the wonder years of childhood and into adulthood, you must take charge, protect your dreams and build your castle one solid brick at a time. You can turn your dreams into a reality.

Remember, too, that there are no shortcuts and you must choose your path wisely. Don't sell out, don't compromise your integrity or your honor, and don't compromise the most important thing in life—your family. (Your family is everything!) Selling or doing drugs is not a career opportunity. It will lead you down a path of self-destruction and cost you your liberty—or worse, quite possibly your life. Gangbanging and violence is not a bullet point on your resume; it's a bullet with your name on it just waiting for someone to pull the trigger. If you mess around on the streets, you run a huge risk of being at the wrong place at the wrong time and getting yourself killed. Please, don't be a statistic! Be careful when choosing your friends, and don't allow people to drag you into the abyss. Get rid of your negative friends before they destroy your mind. It's like I said before, my grandfather was absolutely right when he told me years ago, "You show me your friends, and I'll tell you who you are." Surround yourself with positive people, and reach out to those people who can make you better!

I have never served time in prison (thank God), but I have been busted and been around the block a few times (you DON'T want or need a police record). There is absolutely no glory or nobility in being handcuffed and thrown into the back seat of a squad car, humiliated, while being transported to a police station with no dignity where you'll be booked, photographed and fingerprinted. Not to mention the fact that your name will be all over tomorrow morning's newspaper, letting the whole world know exactly what you've done. I know people (my old friends in low places) who are doing hard time in a federal penitentiary and, believe me, you don't want to end up there. I've seen it, and you don't ever want to be there. EVER!

Some of the so-called smartest people in the world today are in prison. Do you know why? Because they tried beating the system and taking an easier path. I will tell you again: there are no shortcuts! Stealing cars and robbing houses will not make you a successful person, let alone fill you with any appreciation or respect for whatever you stole. Walking is always easy when the road is flat, but true winners make the decision to be a hero and take the high road. It's the more difficult route, but the rewards are definitely worth the effort.

Equal education means equal pay, so stay in school (bright futures are built on a strong education). Stay out of trouble, maintain good grades and go to college to level the playing field. I encourage you to dream and to dream big. You can be whatever you want to be because we are all God's creatures, and that makes us very unique and special. Capitalize on your strengths and work on your weaknesses. Be resourceful, improvise, be accessible (24/7) and most importantly, without question, outwork everyone in sight. You have to believe me—if you work hard, you will be a winner. Be willing to adapt like a chameleon, but don't ever let people use, abuse or take advantage of you. Don't be walking around with blinders on—keep your eyes wide open because there are people out there who are always running a hustle—watch your back. One of the things my mother continues to badger me about to this day is to save money, not just for a rainy day, but for my future. She continues to tell me, "You've got to be thinking a little farther down the road."

Be a thinker, and do not fall prey to believing that good things come to those who wait. The only thing you'll get is someone else's leftover, and nobody deserves sloppy seconds. Nobody!

Think about finance before romance, and **STOP** all the teenage pregnancies. If I knew then what I know now, I could have helped save so many people from becoming addicted to drugs, alcohol, violence and prostitution. The next time you decide to blow cocaine up your nose or overindulge in booze, remember that drug addicts and alcoholics don't get visitation rights. We have young kids, teenagers and adults walking around lost in a culture of darkness, and we need to do something about it. Let's all stand up together and help take care of each other—this is the foundation of how the world was built. Do not be part of the juvenile, public aid, welfare or prison systems. Set an example and then lead by that example. The difference between one person's accomplishments and another's failures is often pure desire and a will to persevere. Failures are necessary because they sharpen your skills, so don't be afraid to embrace the challenges. (Take the shot!)

I wish I could hand you a map and a Bible in case you ever lose your way, but life is not that simple. There will be many, many times in your life when you feel awkward or out of place. Do not allow someone else's ignorance or prejudice to interfere in your quest and dreams for success. Life is a process and you can help—together we can build a better system. Life is not a state of democracy but rather a state of emergency, so challenge yourself from deep inside. Like all of the generations before you, it's your turn. It is your God-given right to live out your hopes for the American dream, so do it now!

Today—right now—is the time for you to take a stand and draw your own deep line in the sand. Make the choice and the decision that this is your time and that you are not going to take no for an answer.

"A journey of a thousand miles begins with a single step."

Have you ever heard that proverb? Think about it. Who knows where you will land if you take that first step, and then another, and then another. It doesn't matter where you are today. What matters is where you will be *someday* and how you are going to get there. Whether you go left or right, make sure you go the "right" way.

You must have clarity of purpose to reach your goals, which means it all begins with a written plan that is detailed, clear and specific. Once you make a decision on which direction you want to go, get EXCITED and be PASSIONATE about it! Emotionally commit to achieving it and do so with conviction. I'm here to tell you that it's not going to be easy, and sometimes you're going to feel like a stranger in your own life. (I know!) But you need to thank your ancestors for allowing you the opportunity to stand on their shoulders so that you could be here today to turn the key that opens the door to a whole new world.

When you take that first step, remember that you're not only fighting for your life, but you are fighting for your lifetime. I want you to prove the haters wrong! Live your life like there is no tomorrow because this life is no dress rehearsal. (You must be ready for prime time!) When you look in the mirror, make sure you both like the person you are and that you are proud of the person looking back at you. Remember, don't let where you came from dictate who you are, but let it be part of who you become. (Respect your roots.)

Whether it is your personal life or your career, try not to burn bridges, because what goes around comes around. Always give your best to lend a helping hand, and if you ever find yourself in a power position or with a platform to make a difference, make sure to reach out—please—especially to those less fortunate than you are. Be nice to everyone, and never refuse to shake a hand or extend a common courtesy because you never know...maybe one day that person you neglected or ignored might be writing his first book, *From the Barrio to the Board Room*.

Thank you for sharing this part of the journey with me. *Que Dios le bendiga* (May God bless you).

Note: I want you to remember, **NEVER BE <u>AFRAID</u> TO <u>TAKE THE SHOT</u>**, because the two greatest days in your life are the day you were born and the day you realized why you were born.

I'm proud to lead by example and tell you that I've closed my business and taken a blind leap of faith to serve a higher purpose. I am now the Founder and Chairman of the Board of From the Barrio Foundation. **(Walk with me.)**

EPILOGUE:

It was about five years ago I was approached by a young man who said to me that my car was phat and he wanted to know how to get one? I asked him what he meant by that and he said, "my car was cool and he wanted to know my secret?" I was driving a brand new black Mercedes Benz at the time.

I invited him in for a beer and at the end of the beer you have to picture this, he had these big brown hungry eyes and asked me again, "so Robert what's your secret?"

I asked him to get a napkin and a pen from the bartender and to write down two words, the first word was hard and the second was work. He looked a little confused, but after looking at the napkin he said "hard work, that's your secret?" I looked him straight in his eyes, smiled and said, "that's the secret."

He put the napkin in his pocket shook my hand and ran out the door like I had given him gold. I watched him get in his car and drive away and I said, "you know, there's a story here and I'm going to do something about it, I'm going to write a book."

And this book is going to teach others that the secrets to success are hard work, determination and education. I wanted this book to be used to inspire and motivate people to make better choices and to help them to use it as a road map to avoid the detours that I took in my life.

So after almost two years, I finally released my book but truly believed at the time that I would simply write my book, put it on the Internet and go back to work. But there was phone call I received three years ago that forever changed my life.

The newspapers had written articles about the release of my Barrio book and a woman who had read one of the articles somehow got my number and called me one morning very early at home. She said "are you Robert Renteria, I said yes, she said, she had just read my article in the paper and had a question for me"?

So I said, "okay, what's that"? Then she paused and I could hear that she started to cry, so after about 15-20 seconds I asked her "what's wrong?

Then she said, I will never forget, she said "Robert where have you been, where have YOU been"?

I remember standing there with chills running up and down my spine realizing that not only was I not done, but also my journey with this book had just begun!

Since that call we have created school based and bible based curriculums that are being used all around the country to teach "From the Barrio to the Board Room" and "Mi Barrio" in schools, social service organizations, youth prisons, jails, churches and various other groups working with youth and adults.

We formed From The Barrio Foundation, a 501 (c) (3) non-profit corporation which is targeted at promoting education, a sense of pride, accomplishment, and self-esteem within the youth of our communities.

The book has been adapted by (RFB&D), Recording for the Blind and Dyslexic, which impacts over 237,000 people around the United States who have reading disabilities or who are visually impaired.

The Barrio book was also released in Spanish to help Latino parents better connect with their children. And after seeing the books being used in middle schools, high schools, colleges and higher education.

I decided that we needed a tool that would reach even the younger ages, so after several long discussions with my publisher Corey Michael Blake, we agreed that a graphic novel/comic book was a must and needed to be developed as soon as possible.

This would become another tool that could help cut the umbilical cord from the gang recruitment happening everyday in all the elementary schools.

A new teaching tool that could literally change the landscape for our youth across America, a tool that we could help exchange for all the guns, knives, drugs, needles, booze and even the cigarettes.

In December 2010 we released Mi Barrio from SmarterComics, a message that represents more than just a comic book with pictures and words, but a burning message of hopes and dreams.

So now, I am dedicating my life to sharing my message all around the world, so that for generations to come and for decades to follow until the end of time, we can help people realize their dreams and to help them reach they're full potential.

As the Founder and Chairman of the Board, for The From the Barrio Foundation, I and the Foundation Board Members are committed to doing our part and to helping lead the way by continuing to create tools and resources that will strongly promote both peace and education for all of us as one race, the human race.

I want all of you to believe in yourselves because you are unique. There have been over 10 billion people who have walked on the face of this earth and there has never been another you.

Please surround yourself around good people who can help elevate you and lift you up so that all of you can spread your wings and fly like the angels God intended you to be!

In life, it doesn't matter how hard we get knocked down, what matters is how many times we can get up and fight.

That being said, the greatest gift I can leave you with today is to tell you, that, yes you can change, yes you can grow and yes, you can be anybody you want to be.

Finally, I want you to believe in God, because if you do, doors will open and your lives will change.

You see, the Barrio books prove, that any little boy and or girl coming from the barrio or a ghetto could one day be a published author. And as we say goodbye for now, my books also prove that dreams do come true, and that dreams are alive and well and living today, right here and right now.

I want all of you to know that I love you and there's nothing you can do about it.

PS. I wish you success and never less!
Long Live the Barrio.........

Always,

—ROBERT J. RENTERIA JR.

About the Author

Robert J. Renteria is a successful businessman turned author of *"From the Barrio to the Board Room"* and *"Mi Barrio,"* who is using his books with youth across America to replace violence, delinquency, gangs and drugs with **education, pride, accomplishment,** and **self esteem.**

Robert, the 2010 Chicago Latino Professional of the Year, has dedicated his life to sharing his story with thousands of others so that they, too, can help break the vicious cycle of poverty through **hard work, determination** and **education.** His books and the accompanying curriculums for both schools and churches, are forming our "leaders of tomorrow" by helping them to find their identity, establish core values, set goals for themselves, prioritize education, and strive to reach their full potential.

Renteria has been the keynote speaker at the Hispanic Heritage Reception for Illinois Secretary of State Jesse White, where he was recognized for his achievements as a civic leader and Latino author. He has also presented at the Illinois Association of School Social Workers, McDonald's Hamburger University, Principal's Partnership (sponsored by Union Pacific Railroad), the Chicago Principals and Administrators Association annual conference, the Hispanic National Bar Association in Chicago, the Illinois Legislative Latino Caucus Foundation, and the Chicago School of Professional Psychology. He has been profiled in major media, including *USA Today, The Wall Street Journal, Investor's Business Daily, The Chicago Sun Times, WGN, Univision,* and *Chicago Public Radio.* Robert is supported by political figures (at the local, state and national level), business owners, corporations, University Professors, and middle and high school teachers and principals who share his universal message that everyone has the right to live the American Dream!

Corey Michael Blake has been communicating creatively for over 15 years, first as the face and voice behind a dozen Fortune 500 and Fortune 100 brands as a commercial and voiceover superstar, then as a film producer and director, as an author and publisher, and now as the creative force revolutionizing the reading experience by combining business, self-help and motivational messages with the comic book and graphic novel format. Corey is the founder and President of Round Table Companies and Writers of the Round Table Press, packaging and publishing titles by best-selling authors Tony Hsieh, Chris Anderson, Marshall Goldsmith, Larry Winget, Tom Hopkins and Robert Renteria. He is the co-author of numerous books, including *"Edge! A Leadership Story"* (Finalist 2008 National Best Books Awards) and *"From the Barrio to the Board Room"* and its companion comic book *"Mi Barrio"* (2010 IPPY Award Winner), which are being used around the country in schools and youth prisons to inspire at-risk youth. Corey's work has been covered by the New York Times, Wall Street Journal, USA Today, Forbes, Inc. Magazine, Wired Magazine, Barron's, Publisher's Weekly, School Library Journal, Fox News, Bloomberg TV, WGN, and Investor's Business Daily. His work has won Addy, Belding, Bronze Lion and London International Advertising awards and he has been published in Writer Magazine, Script Magazine and on StartUp Nation.

FROM THE BARRIO FOUNDATION:

From the Barrio Foundation is an Illinois not-for-profit organization that was formed to help address conditions that help youth and young adults avoid choices that may lead to violence, delinquency, drug use and gangs, while promoting education, valuing a sense of pride and accomplishment, and social values that foster improved self-esteem.

The Barrio Foundation has been built on the core values of:

- **Family** – Valuing the family unit by protecting, honoring, and cherishing family first
- **Education** – The desire to take responsibility for one's own learning
- **Inspiration** – The catalyst that ignites the pursuit of hopes and dreams
- **Hard Work** – The willingness and appreciation for making an honest effort
- **Determination** – The willingness to make the tough, positive choices that build character

Barrio's message of keeping hopes and dreams alive through education, hard work, perseverance, determination, and integrity has reached millions across the United States, and beyond its borders. Through the books, *From the Barrio to the Board Room* and *Mi Barrio*, and the From the Barrio to the Classroom Curriculum, individual vision is being created so a lifetime of personal and professional success can be realized.

Visit www.fromthebarrio.com for more information on From the Barrio Foundation, the books and the curriculum. Please get involved and spread the message!

"Many times the downtrodden living in the ghetto assume their life's path is locked in stone and that there is no escape from their predicament. The main thing about Robert's book is that it furnishes hope! Hope to achieve. Hope to succeed via hard work and tenacity. Hope for the future. Hope for a better life. Hope for happiness. Hope for an education. Hope to live life like the privileged. Hope that everyone can be equal no matter from what station in life they were born to. Robert's book provides impetus and direction."

—BEN HANEY
JUSTICE OF THE PEACE

"I FOUND ROBERT TO BE INSPIRING AND COLLABORATIVE. His story builds practical but powerful connections for students, many who are facing circumstances similar to those he shares in the memoir. Robert's life story reinforces the value of hard work, but also focuses on the power of helping others. It's important to provide mentoring relationships with students and Robert brings the value of positive adult relationships to life on the pages of his memoir."

—NANCY BARTOSZ
ASSISTANT PRINCIPAL, WESTMONT HIGH SCHOOL, WESTMONT, IL

All Materials are available in English and Spanish:

- *From the Barrio to the Board Room*
- *Mi Barrio* from SmarterComics
- *From the Barrio to the Classroom* Curriculum★
- *From the Barrio* Faith Based Curriculum★

★All Curriculum is donated by From the Barrio Foundation and is available (with purchase of books) at no cost to schools, youth prisons, churches and community organizations wishing to use it.

Visit www.fromthebarrio.com for more information and to get involved!